Th
Motor M
of Lincolnshire

CW00665060

VOLUME 1
Motorcycles, cars, and lorries
Made in Lincolnshire

By Stephen Pullen

First Published in Great Britain in 2007 by Tucann Books
Text © Stephen Pullen
All rights reserved
Design © TUCANN*design&print*

ISBN 9781873257760

Produced by: TUCANN*design&print*, 19 High Street, Heighington, Lincoln LN4 1RG
Tel & Fax: 01522 790009 • www.tucann.co.uk

ACKNOWLEDGMENTS AND THANKS

This book would not exist without the help of the following people and organisations, and I really cannot thank them enough. I hope I haven't missed anybody out!

Ray Hooley. For the photo's and information on Ruston & Hornsby's. Thanks Ray!

Michael Worthington-Williams. For the Kendall, Lloyd & Traveller information.

Ray Meggett. The first one to help when I started this project!

David Wilson. For putting me in touch with so many nice people

Adam Smith. Manager, Normanby Hall Country Park, (All the Johnson info)

Nigel Land. Expert on Elswick-Hopper & Torpedo. Thanks Nigel..

John Wilson. North East Lincolnshire Archives.

Eric Croft. For the Clayton's picture and all the other info. Watch this space!

James Taylor. Eagre and Baines.

Paul Williamson. Tomcat Motorsport Limited.

Jeremy Phillips. Founder of Sylva Autokits.

Matt Perrins, Operations Director, Stingray Motorsport, suppliers of Sylva Autokits.

Trevor Pyman and The Ginetta Owners Club.

Ron Otter. Ex-employee of Ruston's.

Allan Creasey. For helping with my Ruston's research.

Mike at Pilbeam Racing Designs.

Jon Day at the National Motor Museum.

Tracey Crawley at Stamford Museum.

Sara Basquill at The Museum of Lincolnshire Life.

Steve Thompson at North Lincolnshire Museum.

Lincolnshire Echo, for putting the word out!

And especially my partner, Sue, for all her help and putting up with me.
Also Rocky the cat for always wanting feeding when I'm really busy!

INTRODUCTION

Looking at what little manufacturing goes on in this county now it does come as a surprise to some people that Lincolnshire was once home to a thriving manufacturing industry. Some industries, such as the making of agricultural machinery, are perhaps unsurprising. But few seem to know of the other products, such as railway locomotives and rolling stock, stationary steam and oil engines, pumps, boilers, cranes, road making machinery, excavators, traction engines and military equipment. Going back to World War One, the first tanks were conceived and built here. Lincolnshire was also an important centre for the construction of aircraft. In fact the Sopwith Camel officially credited with shooting down Manfred Von Richtofen, the Red Baron, was Lincoln made! In World War Two the famous X-Craft midget submarines used to attack and cripple the German battleship Turpitz, were assembled in Gainsborough.

And on top of all this there was, and in a small way still is, a thriving motor industry, producing motorcycles, cars, commercial vehicles and motor components.

The original idea for this book goes back to when I was a motorbike mad ten year old. One day I discovered that there had been a motorbike maker close to where I lived. Not such a big deal if you live in Coventry or Birmingham but, to me living in Lincoln, discovering Lincoln Elk motorcycles was like finding buried treasure! Over the years I collected as much about the firm and machines as I could. But during this research other motorbike makers came to light. This also brought up car and lorry manufacturers. I thought it a shame that, although Lincolnshire's steam engine producers ad been well recorded, very little, if anything has ever been written about any of these motor vehicle makers.

So it seemed right that as I have some information to hand that I include them all in one place. But with scant information available, some of the companies involved may have been missed or not covered as well as I would have liked. But after all these years of research I decided that if I didn't get this book into print and record what I'd found out soon I never would!

I would also like to point out that in the early days of motoring it was common, particularly with regard to motorcycles, for people to buy in all the components required, assemble them and call the resulting machine whatever they liked. This means that an unusual machine may now emerge or someone may be regarded as a vehicle maker in family folklore, when in fact they may have only assembled one machine.

With the loss of these companies, few surviving records and the passing on of the workforce, this first effort could never claim to be a definitive history of the subject. During my research I have had the help of many people who were involved at the time or who are genuine experts on this subject, and I would like to thank them now.

Finally I hope I will be forgiven for any errors. At least I've tried. And therefore I would welcome any additions or corrections for a future revised edition.

Stephen Pullen
North Greetwell,
Lincolnshire
January 2007

ABOUT THE AUTHOR

Stephen Pullen was born in Lincoln in 1967 and apparently could tell the difference between a Morris Oxford and an Austin Cambridge before he was two! However this remarkable brain did not expand to any greatness and only became ever more filled with mechanical trivia! After school, which he disliked completely except for physics and metalwork, he went into the motor trade, which is probably no surprise. After 12 years of doing every job from lorry mechanic (at DMT Transport, now there's a name from Lincolnshire's road haulage past!) to car salesman, he decided to re-train as an electro-mechanical engineer. This was solely a financial decision and he didn't enjoy it much as most of it was far too modern! After working as a draughtsman for a manufacturer of industrial power supplies, which he didn't enjoy and later as a customer service engineer on farm equipment, which he did enjoy as it was far more hands-on (thanks Spaldings!), he went to work for his brother in law's quarrying and security devices business.

Stephen lives in the village of North Greetwell with his partner Sue, and cat Rocky. As far as he is concerned the world revolves around old machinery, particularly old motorbikes, cars, tractors and lorries. He has had several articles published on these subjects but this is his first book.

A percentage of the profits from the sale of each book will be donated to The Lincolnshire Vintage Vehicle Society and to The National Motorcycle Museum.

A.F. (A.T. Fraser Ltd), Sleaford

First appearing in 1971 as the AB1, this Mini based three wheeler actually went on sale as a kit car named the A.F. Spyder. Basically it used a front Mini subframe, complete with Mini engine, gearbox etc, mounted to a monocoque body made from teak and marine plywood. At the rear was a single wheel bolted to Mini rear suspension and a single trailing arm. Kit prices started at £275 but, despite being voted by Motor magazine as Best Fun Car of the decade, very few were ever sold. The company was wound up in 1972, only to be re-started at a new base in Marlborough, Wiltshire, in order to make a revised version. The company finally closed down in 1980.

Alpha Centura, Gainsborough

(Photos courtesy of Complete Kit Car)

Kit car manufacturer set up in 2004 on the Corringham Road Industrial Estate, in order to manufacture a glass fibre bodied sports coupe, called the Juventas. The buyer assembled the kit using mainly Toyota MR2 mechanical components. The only none Toyota parts advertised as being required were the steering rack from a Mini, the radiator from an Austin Metro and the rear lights from a Ford Escort. The kit could be bought in

(Photos courtesy of Complete Kit Car)

stages, but if you bought the whole body, chassis and glass kit in one piece it would set you back £6200. Options were available such as stainless steel twin exhaust silencers at £450, carbon fibre doors at £650 per pair, carbon fibre rear bumper at £495 and powder coated chassis at £195. Purpose made fuel tanks and radiators were also in the options list.

Aveling-Barford Ltd, Grantham

Aveling Barford Ltd was formed in 1933, from the ruins of Agricultural and General Engineers Ltd, better known as A.G.E. This company had been the idea of a Mr Maconochie, who was also a director of the Great Eastern Railway. Worried by the huge expansionist plans of American agricultural machinery companies of the day, he proposed amalgamating twelve smaller companies into a force to be reckoned

The badge used by Aveling Barford was modified slightly from that of the companies predecessor, to become a bit more "heraldic".

6

with. The companies included Charles Burrell & Sons Ltd, Aveling & Porter Ltd, Richard Garratt & Co Ltd and Barford & Perkins Ltd. Unfortunately the company hit financial troubles in 1932 and the receiver was brought in. One of the Barford family, Edward, not wishing to see his family firm disappear, managed to rescue it from the ruins, together with Aveling & Porter, and the company of Aveling-Barford Ltd was born. Neither of the parent companies had any Lincolnshire connections, Aveling & Porter coming from Rochester in Kent and Barford & Perkins from Peterborough. But after the merger they set up just outside Grantham, in a factory provided by Ruston & Hornsby. Over 45,000 tons of stock and equipment had to be transferred up from Kent. Ruston & Hornsby actually had a financial stake in Aveling-Barford Ltd, and supplied the oil engines for their motor road rollers.

The new company kept the rearing horse symbol from the Aveling & Porter days, together with the motto 'Invicta' which basically means 'unconquered'.

Initially just concentrating on what they knew best, road rollers, they soon began diversifying into other areas of earthmoving and construction equipment. They also continued in the manufacture of steam engines and equipment, all the way through until the late 1950's.

During the war, in common with most other engineering works in Britain, the company went over to war work, which included the production of Bren Gun Carriers.

In 1946 a sister company, Barford's of Belton Ltd, was set up to take over the production of Barford's agricultural equipment. This was followed by acquiring a company involved in the manufacture of quarrying and asphalt making machinery and another involved with structural steelwork.

Due to it's contacts within the quarrying and construction industries, the company soon began manufacturing small site dumpers using Fordson tractor engines and gearboxes. In 1939 it added the 'shuttle' dumper to the range, which had a reversible drivers seat and controls.

In 1947 the company made it's first large dump truck This six wheeled

7

lorry had a 12 ton capacity and was fitted with a 6 cylinder Dorman diesel engine giving 128bhp.

In 1957 the 4 wheeled 'SL' series dumper truck was introduced. This was fitted with a Leyland six cylinder diesel engine and again featured reversible controls. This was later developed into a 17 tonner fitted with a 201bhp diesel engine and a 5 speed forward, three speed reverse gearbox.

In 1958 the company introduced it's largest truck to date, the bonneted 'SN' series. This 30 ton machine was available with either a Rolls Royce V8 diesel giving 450bhp or a Cummins 6 cylinder diesel of 335bhp. A six speed gearbox was fitted in both cases. A 35 ton vehicle was introduced shortly after which was available with either the Rolls Royce V8 or a Detroit Diesel 2 stoke engine giving 476bhp.

Aveling Barford SN35 dump truck.

In 1968 the company became part of the Special Products Division of the Leyland Motor Corporation. That year it was recorded that the Grantham works covered an area of 70 acres. It was also noted that, apart from a few special order fitments of propriety power and transmission units, everything except castings, was made on site. Aveling-Barford also had a factory in Newcastle upon Tyne, where some machinery fabrication was carried out. Barford's of Belton had ceased the manufacture of agricultural

The Aveling Barford SR was a smaller version of the SL model. This was fitted with a 126bhp Leyland diesel engine and had reversible controls.

equipment, and was producing the 'shuttle' dumper, which by now had a payload of 2 tons. The company also had overseas subsidiaries in places as far flung as Canada, Australia, France and Rhodesia.

Aveling Barford sold this modified version of the SR for use in mines. The photo clearly shows the reversible controls fitted to these vehicles.

9

Upon becoming part of the Leyland Group, Aveling Barford took over the manufacture of the 6 wheeled 690 'Dumptruk' which had previously been made by another Leyland company, AEC. This road legal lorry was fitted with a 187bhp 6 cylinder Leyland diesel engine and had a payload of 13.8 tons.

Aveling-Barford 690. Originally made by AEC, production was transferred to the Grantham works after Leyland took over. (Photo: Paul Sharp)

In 1970 the 'SN' series trucks were replaced by the five model 'Centaur' range, which had capacities of 25 to 50 tons. The largest model, the Centaur 50, was powered by a General Motors supplied V16 2-stroke diesel engine giving 635bhp and had a fluid/nitrogen suspension system. The Centaur range was updated in the late 1970's and was re-designated the RDO series.

Early in the 1970's Aveling-Barford was transferred within the Leyland group to it's Truck and Bus Division, and shortly afterwards was put up for sale. The next few years through to the 1980's were not kind the Aveling-Barford, particularly when, after leaving British Leyland, foreign investors were involved. In 1988 the company was placed into receivership, where it was bought by Duncan Wordsworth, of the Wordsworth group. The company continued, for a while, to make rigid four wheeled dump trucks up to 65 tonne payload and six wheel articulated vehicles of up to 28 tonnes, all to special order only.

Centaur 50 Ton Truck

The company is now known as Barford Dumpers and is still part of Wordsworth Holdings plc, although they now only manufacture small building site dumpers. The Wordsworth group also manufacture Fruehauf lorry trailers at the Grantham factory.

Baines Ltd, Gainsborough

Brothers, Edward and Frank Baines, set up a company as bicycle makers and repairers in 1886. The bicycles they made were sold under the brand name of Aegir (in later advertising spelt as Eagre), which is the name of the tidal flow on the river Trent. In 1900 they announced a new design of light car with a tubular steel frame and fitted with a De Dion-Bouton engine of 2½ Horsepower. The car was to have belt drive but, despite a projected sales price of £100, it was never produced.

Also around the turn of the century it was reported in the press that Frank Baines had made a motorcycle of entirely his own design, except for the engine, which was a 1¾hp De Dion unit. A 28" front wheel and 26" rear were fitted, and there were no bicycle type pedals. The rear wheel ran on double row ball bearings with hinged spherical cages, which allowed the rear wheel to be removed without disturbing the setup. It was reported that the engine had been modified to put the valve chamber in front of the

11

1920 Eagre (Photo: David Wilson)

engine to reduce it's width. The spark plug was also moved to underneath the valve box to reduce the length of sparkplug lead required and help prevent ignition troubles. A jet carburettor was fitted, but as it did not have a float chamber it used an overflow system. A pedal operated friction clutch was also fitted to allow a free engine. Unusually the seat tube was also the exhaust silencer! Apparently it worked perfectly and did not get too hot, so caused no 'discomfort at the saddle'!

There is no record of this machine having gone into production, and may have been just for Frank Baines' personal use. However some years later the company again marketed a machine under the Eagre name, but only for one week in November 1920! This machine was a lightweight model fitted with a 349cc Precision two stroke engine, driving through a chain driven Sturmey-Archer two speed gearbox and Brammer vee-belt to the rear wheel. Little more is known about the production of this machine, but it is believed very few were made. It also appears that production stopped due to the engine maker, Precision, being taken over by the Beardmore group of companies in 1920, and going into full scale motorcycle production themselves as Beardmore-Precision.

One machine still exists, having been discovered in 1979 in a barn in the village of Cottam by Vintage Motorcycle Club founder Titch Allen. It was then bought and restored to it's current superb condition by Albert Hull.

It must be noted that Frank Baines also worked with R. M Wright on the sales of Stonebow cars, and that both Baines Brothers were involved with the designing of cars for Rose Brothers (See National).

BRM Ltd (British Racing Motors Ltd), Bourne and Folkingham
(See also ERA and Raymond Mays)

In 1933 Raymond Mays, a leading amateur racing driver had co-founded English Racing Automobiles (ERA), to produce and race cars in the voiturette class. However he had long held the ambition to construct a serious British Grand Prix car. So in 1945, together with ERA collaborator Peter Berthon, Mays launched an appeal for financial support. By 1946 over one hundred companies had announced that they would back the project. 1947 saw the formation of the British Motor Racing Research Trust to assist with the project and the company to build the cars was renamed, from Automobile Developments Ltd, to British Racing Motors Ltd on the 15th of December 1949. BRM was born! The workshops for the new company were set up at Folkingham airfield just north of Bourne, which was also used as a test track. As the company expanded the main factory moved to Spalding Road in Bourne, but testing was still carried out at Folkingham.

Due to the state of the economy at that time, with material shortages etc, the first car was not completed and shown to the public until December 1949. The body consisted of a tubular steel chassis frame with a light aluminium alloy body. The fuel tanks were also aluminium. Front suspension was by trailing arms with Lockheed pneumatic struts. Rear suspension was a de Dion axle, single radius rods and Lockheed pneumatic struts. Braking was by Girling three-shoe brakes, and transmission was by a triple plate clutch and five speed gearbox, mounted transversally at the rear. Braking was later uprated to Girling discs. A limited slip differential was also fitted. The engine was an extremely complicated V16 unit designed by Peter Berthon and Eric Richter. With 1496cc, twin overhead camshafts per cylinder bank, a two-piece ten bearing crankshaft and a two stage centrifugal supercharger made by Rolls-Royce, it's claimed power output was 430bhp at 11,000rpm.

Two cars were entered for the Daily Express Trophy race at Silverstone in August 1950. Unfortunately during testing both cars suffered cracked cylinder liners, so only one made it to the start line. Much was expected of this British wonder car. So when the driver, Raymond Sommer, let out the clutch only for a half-shaft to break, people were not happy. The car was jeered and some of the crowd threw pennies at it.

1950 BRM V16 (National Motor Museum)

One of two lightweight prototypes made by BRM in 1953 to test components for the new 2½ litre formula of 1954. Became known as the Mk2. (National Motor Museum)

14

The following month things looked up, when Reg Parnell drove it at Goodwood, and won two short races. This, however was to be the only high spot for quite a while.

The next two years proved a catalogue of disasters for BRM, and despite employing the likes of Fangio and Moss to drive for them, they had very little success.

In October 1952 Alfred Owen, of the Rubery Owen organisation, took over the company. The car was continually developed and it is claimed that by mid 1953 the engine was developing 585bhp at 11,800rpm.

However, in 1953 it was announced that the Grand Prix Formula for the following year would be for 2½ litres cars. So BRM built two lightweight Mk2 versions of the V16, in order to develop components for the new formula. With a space frame chassis, smaller wheels and a shorter chassis, it actually proved to be an acceptable car, winning it's first ever race, at the Goodwood Easter meeting in April 1954.

1959 BRM Type 25 (National Motor Museum)

The car that BRM developed for the new formula was the Type 25. A completely new car, it was fitted with a 2497cc, four cylinder engine, with a power output of 248bhp at 9,000rpm, in it's original form. The transmission was a four speed crash gearbox, of BRM's own design, that was in unit with the final drive. The body consisted of a tubular steel space frame chassis skinned in magnesium alloy. Rear suspension was by twin radius arms each side and oleo-pneumatic struts, and a de Dion axle located by a parallel link motion running from the nearside hub to the chassis. The front was by unequal length double wishbones and oleo-pneumatic struts. Braking was by Lockheed, with a single transmission disc brake operating on the gearbox output shaft. In 1957, on the advice of Colin Chapman of Lotus, coil springs were fitted all round. 1957 also saw a slightly revised body, with higher cockpit sides and wrap around Perspex windscreen. 1958 saw more improvements, with a lighter and stronger space frame chassis and revised front suspension.

Despite all these improvements, the Type 25's performance could best be described as disappointing. In fact it would be May 1959 before one, driven by Joakim Bonnier, scored a victory by winning the Dutch GP.

At the Italian GP in 1959, BRM unveiled a rear engined prototype, the Type 48. Useful as a test-bed, it was completely outclassed by the competition, particularly from Cooper.

In 1960 new workshops were built for BRM for racing car preparation, on the site of Bourne's old gas works.

For 1961 the Grand Prix Formula was again changed, this time to un-supercharged cars of between 1301 and 1500cc. With a bit of a 'head in the sand' attitude, BRM decided that by not developing a new car they could persuade the governing body to keep the existing rules. Surprisingly, this plan did not work, and BRM ended up fitting a Coventry-Climax FPF 4 cylinder engine, that had been introduced in 1957, into a Mark 2 version of the Type 48 car. However, as this had been designed originally for a 2½ litre engine it was rather heavy and results for 1961 were therefore very disappointing.

In 1962 there was another new car, and this proved the turning point in BRM's fortunes. Dubbed the Type 57, it was powered by a 1498cc V8,

16

with twin overhead camshafts per cylinder bank and Lucas fuel injection. Power output was 184bhp at 10,000rpm. This was increased with continual development. With this car Graham Hill won the 1962 World Championship, with a twelve point margin over Jim Clark, and BRM also won the Constructors Championship!

L. Bandini taking part in the 1963 British GP in a BRM P57. (National Motor Museum)

1963 was again quite successful, with Hill taking second place in the Drivers Championship. Although relying on the type 57, a new car was produced, the semi-monocoque Type 61, which was very much a stop gap experimental model. BRM also collaborated with Rover to produce and race the Rover-BRM gas turbine car at Le Mans. It must be remembered that, at the time, Rover was very much a very forward thinking company. The complete opposite to later years....

For 1964 the mark 2 version of the Type 61, the 261, was introduced. Using the now familiar V8 engine, the car was now fully developed into a full monocoque. Again BRM did very well, and Graham Hill was pipped at the post for World Champion due to an unfortunate minor accident in the last race of the season.

1964 also saw the arrival of another interesting car, the Type 67. Designed by Mike Pilbeam (See Pilbeam Racing Designs), it was unusual as it was fitted with a Ferguson four wheel drive system. Although it practiced for the 1964 British GP, it did not actually race. However in 1968 it was used by Peter Lawson to capture the 1968 British Hill Climb Championship.

17

Rear view of a 1966 BRM Type P83 fitted with the complex 3 litre H16 engine. Note the exhaust systems! (National Motor Museum)

Yet again the racing governing body announced a change in the GP formula. For 1966 the cars would be up to 3 litres. The car BRM designed was supposed to have a very long development life ahead of it, but instead proved extremely troublesome. The new engine they designed was in an H16 layout, which had two horizontally opposed banks of eight cylinders,

A BRM P83 in the hands of Jackie Stewart in the 1967 Belgian Grand Prix. (National Motor Museum)

18

1968 BRM P133 (National Motor Museum)

giving a total of 2,999cc. Using a six speed gearbox, the chassis was a development of the Type 61 Mark 2. Christened the Type 83, the car's H16 engine proved extremely complicated and unreliable. So much so that BRM was sometimes forced to used the old V8 bored out to two litres instead!

By 1968 BRM had had enough of trying to cure the H16's problems, and a new car was introduced, the V12 P126. To speed up development the design and construction of the first car was contracted out. All subsequent cars were made at the Bourne works, and were designated as P133's. The V12 engine used had a capacity of 2999.5cc and a claimed power output of 400bhp, and drove through a five speed Hewland gearbox.

Following mediocre success in 1968, a new version, the P139, was introduced in 1969. Basically the same as a P133, it now had a BRM designed gearbox and four valves per cylinder, which increased the power to a claimed 450bhp. However, once again, the racing results were disappointing.

1970 saw a new car, the P153, designed for the V12 engine. This car brought BRM a much needed victory, when Pedro Rodriguez won the Belgian GP.

Sticking with the V12 engine, BRM introduced the P160 for the 1971 season. This had improved suspension, and more power. This car brought the team two GP victories during the year.

Jackie Oliver driving a BRM P160B in the British GP of 1972. (National Motor Museum)

A BRM P180 of 1972. (National Motor Museum)

The P160 was improved for 1972 and re-named the P160B. Team tactics changed also, and it was announced that at most races six cars would be entered! In reality it was never more than five. Fortunes did not improve however, and the season was a disaster. The only high spot being the win at Brands Hatch in October by another new car, the P180. Surprisingly, the car was dropped at the end of the season.

1973 brought more improvements to the P160, now called the P160E. However, the year turned out to be another string of retirements and low placed finishes.

A new car for 1974, the P201, should have helped. But yet again the results were poor.

In December of that year Rubery Owen finally lost patience with BRM, and the company was wound up. However it was taken over by Louis Stanley, and 1975 saw one P201 car entered for some races as the Stanley-BRM, but without success. 1976 saw the introduction of the equally disappointing P207 and 1978 saw the final BRM, the P230. It was made for BRM by CTG Racing of Ferndown, and was only sent to Bourne for finishing off. 1978 was to show no success and turned out to be BRM's last season.

1975 V12 BRM P201 (National Motor Museum)

21

Clayton Electric wagon. Made 1919 - 1930. (Eric Croft)

Clayton & Shuttleworth Ltd and Clayton Wagons Ltd, Lincoln

In 1842 Nathaniel Clayton left his position as master of the Lincoln to Boston steam packet Countess of Warwick, in order to set up a small iron foundry on a one acre site on the south bank of the river Witham in Lincoln. His first contract of any importance was the casting of iron pipes for Lincoln's water supply. Adjoining the foundry was a boatbuilding business which was part owned by Clayton's son-in-law, Joseph Shuttleworth. Later that year they decided to go into partnership in order to manufacture steam engines and agricultural equipment such as threshing machines, saw benches and flour mills. The company prospered and by the time of Joseph's death in 1883 over 25,000 engines had been produced, the main works had grown to over 20 acres and the company had branches all over the world.

Clayton and Shuttleworth Ltd entered the world of the internal combustion engine during the First World War when they began to assemble aircraft, such as the famous Sopwith Camel and Vickers Vimy, for the Ministry of War. In 1916 they were also awarded a contract by the Ministry of Food, to design and manufacture a batch of petrol driven crawler tractors rated at thirty-five horsepower. As well as farm work, some of these tractors also saw service with the British Army in France.

After seeing the potential of internal combustion, the company briefly experimented with building a petrol engined lorry, using components from the five ton steam wagons they produced. However, upon cessation of hostilities, they surprised everyone by introducing a range of battery electric lorries, for loads from two up to six tons. Ideal for town work, some of the biggest users were local authorities who bought them for refuse collection work. These lorries were built in the Titanic Works, alongside the company's steam wagons, from 1919 all the way through until 1930.

In 1926 Clayton and Shuttleworth Ltd went into liquidation and all manufacturing was taken over a subsidiary company, Clayton Wagons Ltd, which had been set up in 1917 to manufacture railway equipment. Over the next few years many assets were sold off, including Clayton Forge to Thomas Smith of Coventry in 1929 and the Titanic Works were taken over by Clayton Dewandre Co Ltd in 1928. This firm went on in later years to dominate fields such as commercial vehicle braking. But in 1930, just four years after their last troubles the company again found itself in financial difficulties and was again placed into liquidation. This time there was to be no reprieve and the company was closed with patent rights being sold off, principally to Marshalls, Sons & Co Ltd of Gainsborough. The name finally disappeared in 1936. It is interesting to note that Marshall's, after acquisition of the Clayton company rights, actually badged some of their tractors as Clayton's for export markets.

At their height Clayton and Shuttleworth employed over 5,000 people and owned four separate factories in Lincoln, these being Stamp End Works, Clayton Forge, Titanic Works and Abbey Works.

Eagre, Gainsborough

See Baines Ltd

Elswick-Hopper Cycle & Motor Company, Barton-on-Humber

In 1880 an ex Marshall's, Sons & Co engineer named Fred Hopper decided to set up as a bicycle repairer in a former blacksmith's shop on Brigg Road, Barton on Humber. At some point just prior to 1890 he decided to start manufacturing of bicycles. The company flourished and moved into new premises on Marsh Lane. In 1904 Fred Hopper decided to enter the motorcycle world by importing German NSU machines and by 1906 was offering two twin cylinder machines of 4hp and 5½ hp respectively. Both models used 20 inch frames and 24 inch wheels. The 4hp machine had a list price of £35 and 14 shillings. In 1907 the range of imports was increased to include four different single cylinder tourers, three twins and a lightweight machine of 1¼hp.

In 1908 the largest and smallest singles were dropped from the range and all NSU motorcycles sold by Hopper from then on were badged as Torpedo's, which is the name Hopper had given to all the top of the range bicycle models his company manufactured.

In 1909 Hopper decided to add a car to the Torpedo range, but the 6hp De Dion engined single cylinder model sold was in fact made by the Star Cycle Company of Wolverhampton, and only badged as a Torpedo. Torpedo cars were only offered for a couple of years but the later models (also made by Star) had twin cylinders.

1910 was an important year for Hopper. Firstly he decided stop importing NSU motorcycles and instead design and manufacture his own Torpedo motorcycle. Secondly he purchased the assets of the Newcastle based Elswick Cycle Company Ltd, in order to be able to manufacture an additional range of bicycles and motorcycles. A new company was formed and named the Elswick-Hopper Cycle and Motor Company, and all manufacturing was to be done at Barton upon Humber. It must be noted that although Elswick had marketed cars from 1903 until 1907, there was no connection between the Elswick car models and the subsequent Torpedo car. The Elswick car had in fact been made by an unknown London maker and re-badged.

The new Torpedo motorcycle used a Fafnir single cylinder four stroke engine of 80mm bore and 90mm stroke. Magneto ignition and spring forks were standard. Rated at 4¼hp it sold to the trade at £35. However by the Olympia Exhibition in November 1910 this machine had been dropped and two new models were on display, these being a standard 3½hp and a 2hp lightweight. The engines were now supplied by Precision, and this engine maker would be used exclusively by Hopper from now on.

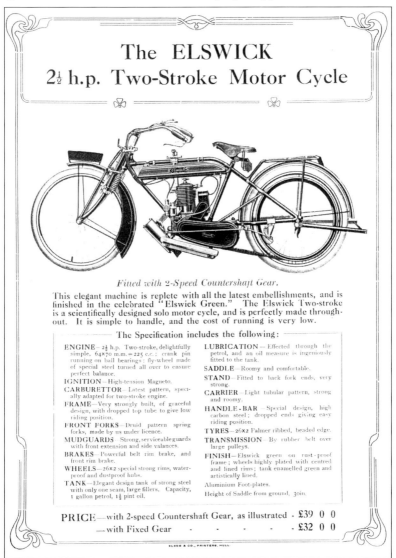

The ELSWICK
2¼ h.p. Two-Stroke Motor Cycle

Fitted with 2-Speed Countershaft Gear.

This elegant machine is replete with all the latest embellishments, and is finished in the celebrated "Elswick Green." The Elswick Two-stroke is a scientifically designed solo motor cycle, and is perfectly made throughout. It is simple to handle, and the cost of running is very low.

The Specification includes the following:

ENGINE—2¼ h.p. Two-stroke, delightfully simple, 64×70 m.m. = 225 c.c.; crank pin running on ball bearings; fly-wheel made of special steel turned all over to ensure perfect balance.

IGNITION—High-tension Magneto.

CARBURETTOR—Latest pattern, specially adapted for two-stroke engine.

FRAME—Very strongly built, of graceful design, with dropped top tube to give low riding position.

FRONT FORKS—Druid pattern spring forks, made by us under licence.

MUDGUARDS—Strong, serviceable guards with front extension and side valances.

BRAKES—Powerful belt rim brake, and front rim brake.

WHEELS—26×2 special strong rims, waterproof and dustproof hubs.

TANK—Elegant design tank of strong steel with only one seam, large fillers. Capacity, 1 gallon petrol, 1½ pint oil.

LUBRICATION—Effected through the petrol, and an oil measure is ingeniously fitted to the tank.

SADDLE—Roomy and comfortable.

STAND—Fitted to back fork ends, very strong.

CARRIER—Light tubular pattern, strong and roomy.

HANDLE-BAR—Special design, high carbon steel; dropped ends giving easy riding position.

TYRES—26×2 Palmer ribbed, beaded edge.

TRANSMISSION—By rubber belt over large pulleys.

FINISH—Elswick green on rust-proof frame; wheels highly plated with centred and lined rims; tank enamelled green and artistically lined.

Aluminium Foot-plates.

Height of Saddle from ground, 30in.

PRICE—with 2-speed Countershaft Gear, as illustrated - £39 0 0
—with Fixed Gear - - - - - £32 0 0

ELSOM & CO., PRINTERS, HULL.

At the following year's Olympia Exhibition two models were again displayed, these being a 3½hp roadster and a 2½hp lightweight. Quickly detachable front mudguards and a cable operated clutch were items of note on the new machines. As an example of the reliability of these machines, a Mr Clark went on to win gold medals in both the 1913 and 1914 'London-Land's End-London' trials riding the same 3½hp machine!

Elswick motorcycles were also on display, the first time since Hopper's takeover. To keep up the appearance of Elswick being a separate company it had a separate stand from Torpedo. Two Elswick's were on display, a standard 3¾hp single with clutch operated two speed gearbox, and a 2½hp lightweight. Both machines were painted traditional Elswick green.

An Elswick 3½hp of 1913. Only four Elswicks are known to survive from this period. (Photo Keith Fryer)

Between 1911 and 1912 separate workshops were built for Torpedo and Elswick in Barton on Humber, and reported combined output for the two marques was 718 machines for 1911/12 trading period. However the cost of these new buildings and the required new machinery caused severe cash flow problems. This lead to a group of suppliers taking legal action against Elswick-Hopper and the company was placed into receivership in 1913. However the company was re-structured and continued trading.

By 1913 Hopper were reported as making Druid forks under licence and had also patented a compensating device for rear brakes to increase braking efficiency and provide even wearing of the friction material.

The Torpedo Motor Cycle Set

Many Traders prefer to assemble motorcycles with engines, etc., of their own selection, and, in this way, secure a good profit whilst building up for themselves an ' Own-name ' connection and goodwill which can never be taken away from them. The frame illustrated takes any standard engine and makes up into an exceedingly attractive motorcycle. If you have not already handled motorcycles, **start to-day.** We were the pioneers of the Agents' ' Own-transfer ' cycle, and we are offering Agents the same opportunity as we did in the early days of the pedal cycle.

The illustration shews the celebrated 2¼ h.p. Motorcycle, complete as specification, with nothing further required but the power unit, tyres, etc.

When you have fitted the necessary parts you have ready for sale a Motorcycle forwhich you will find ready customers, leaving you a handsome margin of profit, as well as being the means of building up a reputation for high-class goods of your own manufacture.

SPECIFICATION.

Correctly designed Light-weight frame, built with accurately machined lugs and best weldless steel tubing; head is fitted with one-piece webbed head lug and lengthened to give easy steering; spring forks made in our own works under ' Druid ' licence; wheels built with strong gauge rims for 26 × 2in. beaded edge tyres, double-butted spokes; belt rim fitted to take ⅞in. belt; wide mudguards, handlebar complete with grips, exhaust lifter lever and wire, and front rim brakes; belt rim brake with patented compensating device and with operating pedal; pedalling gear with Perry's chain; sheet steel tank made with only one seam and fitted with safety division between oil and petrol compartments; oil pump; petrol gauge; magneto advance lever; and finished in aluminium with black panels and lined; seat pillar; back carrier; back wheel stand, and number plates. Beautifully finished in Electric Black, and hand-polished. All bright parts plated on copper.

Price .. .. .. £10 10 0 Ledger Account.

Special Nett Cash with Order, Price £9 10 0

Delivery F.O.R. Barton-on-Humber. Crates charged extra.

Page from an Elswick-Hopper Torpedo brochure showing the kit of parts available to the trade allowing them to make their own motorcycles. This was a very common practice and leads to some identification problems today!

For the 1915/16 trading year Hopper announced that six Torpedo models would be available, these being two lightweight four strokes of 2hp and 2½hp respectively, a 2½hp two stroke, a 3hp tourer, a 4hp twin and a 4½hp sidecar combination.

The same six Torpedo machines were still listed in 1918, but a note on the price list stated that they were 'withdrawn temporarily' as the company were not in a position to fulfil orders due to war contracts. These war contracts included the manufacture of forks for Ariel and machine gun mountings for BSA. These contracts proved very profitable for the company and were very welcome after Elswick-Hopper's pre-war financial problems.

After the war production continued, but it was obvious motorcycle production was running down. A report on the Olympia Exhibition by the Motor Cycle magazine of the 27th of November 1919 stated that there was only one Elswick and one Torpedo on display, and they were both identical except for the paint finish. Both were 3½hp two stroke's with wet sump lubrication. Specification included 2 speed Sturmey-Archer gearboxes with kick starters and Brampton Biflex spring forks. In fact it is believed that the post war machines were just an effort to use up pre-war stocks of parts, as Hopper had decided to return to just bicycle manufacture.

The only surviving Elswick VAP prototype. (Photo Mark Daniels)

No motor cycles were produced after 1919, but the bicycle company thrived and was listed on the London Stock Exchange in 1936. The successor company to Elswick-Hopper, Falcon Cycles, continues to make bicycles in the Lincolnshire town of Brigg.

However in 1953 Elswick-Hopper did have one final venture into the motorcycle world when they were approached by Trojan to design and manufacture a frame for testing a new moped engine. Unfortunately, despite successful trials, the Trojan engine project ended in failure. However the project raised Elswick's interest in producing a moped of their own. By 1958 an Elswick frame fitted with a Dunkley engine was under trial, but this proved unreliable. The next engine to be tried was the French made VAP type 57, which was far better. Six prototypes were made and they spent a week being tested at the MIRA test facility in Warwickshire. Five survived unscathed, but one suffered a brazing fracture.

So with a successful trial the machine was re-styled for production, and was named the Lynx. Two machines were displayed at the Motor Cycle Show at Earls Court in 1960 alongside a range of imported mopeds which were to be sold by the Scootermatic company. This company had been set up by Elswick to handle sales of Auto-Vap, Capri, Como, Laverda and Velo-Vap machines, as well as the Lynx. Unfortunately the Lynx machine was dropped as it was found it could not be made and sold at a competitive price.

The Elswick made Lynx. (Photo Mark Daniels)

As an aside Elswick turned down the chance to become the sole UK importers of the Honda 50, and this decision was taken in spite of extensive testing. The Honda design went on to spawn the C70 and C90, and became the world's best selling motorcycle of all time. The Elswick-Hopper choice sank without trace. We can only wonder at what might have been…

Both Lynx machines still survive as does the number five MIRA test machine.

ERA, (English Racing Automobiles) Bourne
(See also Raymond Mays and BRM)

The man behind ERA, and later BRM, was Thomas Raymond Mays who was born in the market town of Bourne, South Lincolnshire, in 1899. He was the son of a local businessman and Justice of the Peace, Mr T.W. Mays. From an early age Raymond became fascinated by his father's Vauxhall and Napier cars and this interest was helped by the fact that his father was also interested in cars and entered them in hill climbs and speed trials.

In December 1917 Raymond joined the Army, and went to the Guards Officers Training Establishment at Bushy Hill. After training he joined the Grenadier Guards, and served first in a home posting, but he soon found himself in France. At the end of the war he was then posted to the army of occupation in Germany.

In 1919 he resigned his commission, and went to Cambridge University to read engineering. Here he joined the Cambridge University Auto Club, and took part in his first motor race, in a Hillman which he named 'Quick Silver'. Bitten by the motor racing bug, this was to be the start of his new life.

After leaving university, Raymond went to work in the family business, but continued motor racing in his spare time, driving cars made by Bugatti, Vauxhall, A.C, Mercedes Benz and Invicta. He also modified and sold Buggati cars as "The Raymond Mays Type super-sports Brescia." This featured a special camshaft, pistons and magneto to give a top speed of "rather more than 90mph, depending on conditions."

A rolling chassis with these modifications would set you back £500, or £550 if you wanted a body fitting.

In 1933 he took delivery of a new six cylinder Riley, which after much development took Mays to many 1500cc class wins. The car became quite famous and was known as the 'White Riley'.

A 'Raymond Mays' Type Super-Sports Brescia Bugatti, on display at the Bourne Motorsport Memorial day. (Photo Darren Pullen)

Another driver and racing enthusiast, Humphrey Cook, was so impressed with the performance of the White Riley that he contacted Mays with a view to constructing a new 'voiturette' class (pre-war equivalent of Formula Two) racing car based on it. Mays was very enthusiastic about the idea and so he and Cook came to an agreement and formed the company of English Racing Automobiles Ltd. Cook became principle shareholder and managing director, whilst Mays and Peter Berthon, engineer & fellow enthusiast, became directors with a nominal shareholding. The company started production in a workshop built on what had been the orchard behind May's house in Bourne.

Using some of Berthon's ideas the chassis for the new car was designed by Reid Railton, of Thomsom & Taylor of Brooklands. In later years Railton designed the Napier-Railton land speed record car for John Cobb. The design he came up with for the ERA was extremely simple. A channel section frame with semi-eliptic springs and rigid axles. The engine fitted was a heavily modified Riley six cylinder unit, with an aluminium cylinder head and a Rootes type supercharger. At 1488cc it gave 150bhp at 6,500rpm. The transmission was a pre-selector unit made by Armstrong-Siddeley. Designated the 'A' type, it's top speed was around 125mph.

It's first outing was to have been a race in the Isle of Man in May 1934, however serious handling problems showed up in practice, so the car was withdrawn. But by the time of that year's British Empire Trophy Race at Brooklands, the car was ready, with the handling problem sorted by the fitting of new rear springs and modifications to the steering. Unfortunately the car was unclassified, as it seemed to spend most of the race in the pits having one small problem sorted after another.

By the August Bank Holiday meeting at Brooklands, ERA had produced a second car, this one fitted with a smaller 1088cc engine developing 140bhp. This car, driven by Humphrey Cook, brought ERA's first ever victory in a short handicap race. Mays, driving the 1488cc car, finished second in another race. Also that month both cars set new International class records for both the standing start kilometre and mile, using the Railway Straight at Brooklands.

ERA R3A on display at the Bourne Motorsport Memorial day on the 29th of August 1999. This 2 litre car was built in 1934 and was used by Raymond Mays to set the Outright World Standing Start Kilometre record. (Photo Darren Pullen)

Two more cars were constructed in 1934, a 1950cc and another 1088cc. The racing performances for the rest of the year proved so promising, that ERA decided to take on races abroad during 1935. So the car was slightly re-designed, with extra chassis bracing, different gearbox ratios and different rear springs. This car was christened the 'B' type.

1935 proved extremely profitable for ERA, not only from a racing point of view but also for sales. Cars were sold, with a list price of £1050, to some of the most famous names in pre-war racing, including Prince Birabongse of Siam, who raced as B. Bira, Dick Seaman, and Lord Howe. Racing victories included The Nuffield Trophy at Donington Park, the Voiturette race at Dieppe and the Circuit of Masaryk Voiturette race at Brno in Czechoslovakia.

Raymond Mays driving an ERA R4B (National Motor Museum)

1936 brought the company more success, and by the end of the year ERA announced a new car for 1937, the 'C' type. Up to this point total ERA production stood at four 'A' types and thirteen 'B' types.

The 'C' type car was really just a modified 'B' type. Changes included a stronger box section chassis, Lockheed hydraulic brakes, a limited slip differential, and Porsche trailing link and torsion bar independent front suspension. Girling Luvax hydraulic dampers were fitted, instead of the friction dampers fitted to the previous models. A Zoller vane type supercharger was also specified as standard, and the connecting rods were strengthened. All these modifications brought the power of the 1500cc version of the car up to 240bhp at 7500rpm, and gave a top speed of 140mph. In reality only three cars were made to 'C' type specification, and all were just existing 'B' types given the new modifications.

1937 and 1938 proved just as fruitful for the ERA's as regards racing, and success came at races all over Britain, Europe and even in South Africa.

1938 saw Mays up-rate his car heavily, and this became known as the 'D' type. The modifications done by Mays included a lighter chassis, due to extensive drilling of the side rails, extra Girling Luvax dampers, shortened front trailing arms and external radius arms to the back axle, to prevent axle judder under braking.

In 1939 ERA could see that a new car was needed if they were to remain competitive, particularly in the light of new offerings from Alfa-Romeo and Maserati. ERA's answer was the 'E' type. Originally conceived as a Grand Prix car, it had been abandoned due to lack of funds. Still using a Riley based six cylinder engine of 1487cc, it had a Zoller vane type supercharger, twin choke SU carburettor and wet sump lubrication. It had a power output of 260bhp at 7,500rpm. The body and chassis were

ERA E-Type racing at Castle Donington (National Motor Museum)

34

a complete departure from the previous models, incorporating a tubular steel frame and a low, sleek body. It was entered, with Mays as driver, for an International Trophy race at Brooklands at Easter 1939. Unfortunately the car required far more development and was withdrawn.

1939 also saw company problems. Humphrey Cook had been ERA's financial backer since it started, but decided he could no longer continue in this role on his own. So a public subscription was launched with the intention of raising £8,000. Unfortunately this idea failed, so Cook decided the company should be closed. However before this could happen ERA was taken on by the British Motor Racing Fund. It was at this point that Mays tendered his resignation and left the company. Cook stayed on to run the company for the new owners, and the works were transferred from Bourne to Donington Park in Derbyshire. New cars continued to be produced, and the company finally withdrew from racing in 1952.

Gainsborough Motor Engineering Co Ltd, Gainsborough

Between 1902 and 1903 this company made a small number of cars fitted with 16 horsepower, 4 cylinder horizontal engines, which were mounted beneath the vehicle floor. The engine seems to have been extremely complex in that it had external connecting rods fixed to a shaft which passed transversely through the piston and cylinder and conveyed the power to the crankshaft. Fitted with a chain driven two speed gearbox, it's final drive was also by chain. The body was a four seat tonneau, which the company called the Duchess. The rear section of the body could be converted into a closed brougham.

Ginetta Cars Limited, Scunthorpe

Ginetta Cars Limited was formed in 1958 by the four Walklett brothers to manufacture two seater sports kit cars from a factory at Witham in Essex. In 1968 the company had it's G15 model type approved, allowing it to be sold either as a kit or as a fully assembled vehicle. This was followed by type approval of it's G21 in 1970. In order to start large scale production of these cars, the company moved to a purpose built factory in Suffolk in 1972. However, the company hit financial troubles due to the oil crisis of the early 70's and the introduction by the British government of value added tax. In order to save the company production was returned to Witham in 1974. Kit production was once again top priority.

1990 Ginetta G32 convertible (Malcolm Harrison)

The company grew and in 1989 decided to once again enter the type approved production car market and therefore moved to a factory on Dunlop Way, Scunthorpe, in order to manufacture their new model, the G32. This car was a mid-engined two seater using most of it's mechanical components from the Ford Fiesta XR2 parts bin. The engine chosen was a 1.6 litre CVH injection unit from a Ford Escort XR3i. The doors were also Fiesta, but were cut down to fit the lower body height of the Ginetta.

Later in 1989 the company was purchased by a group of businessmen led by Martin Phaff and Mike Modiri. Three of the Walklett brothers retired and the other brother, Ivor, who had been Ginetta's designer, became the new company's technical director.

In 1990 a convertible version of the G32 was introduced which was mechanically the same as the coupe. Also in 1990 two experimental G32's were made which were fitted with Ford RS1600 Turbo engines, but this version was never put into production due to cooling problems. There was, however, a high performance version introduced fitted with a 1.9 litre fuel injected Ford CVH engine made by Specialised Engines in Essex.

In 1991 the G33 was introduced. This was a front engined, rear wheel drive, open topped sports car with pop-up headlamps. The engine chosen for this car was the Rover V8, in 3.9 litre, fuel injected guise, coupled to a five speed Rover manual gearbox, and driving through a Sierra Cosworth rear differential. This car had a claimed top speed of 150mph and a 0-60mph time of 5.3 seconds.

1991 Ginetta G33 (Courtesy Ginetta Owners Club)

37

G32 production ended in December 1992, when 110 fixed head coupes and 20 convertibles had been made. The following year production of the G33 was moved away from the county.

The company survives and now manufactures cars in Sheffield, South Yorkshire as part of the LNT Group.

Glanford, Brigg

In 1904 a Brigg bicycle maker named George Henry Laynes, originally from Winterton near Scunthorpe, assembled a small quantity of motorcycles and sold them under the name Glanford. Nothing else known.

Grimsby, Grimsby

Cleethorpes garage proprietor, Fred Lloyd (see Lloyd) is recorded as holding an agency for this make in 1920. Nothing else known.

Hayes & Son, Stamford

Motor vehicle body makers. See Pick/New Pick

Johnson, Scunthorpe

In 1890 George James Bell Johnson returned to his home town of Scunthorpe, after several years working in the bicycle industry all over Britain. He had started with an apprenticeship at the Burton Cycle Machine Company in Warrington, Lancashire. During his time at Burton's he also became quite a successful cycle racer, and set many records in the then popular town to town races. Unfortunately for George, Burtons suffered a major fire, and he found himself out of work. So, deciding he wanted to stay in the world of bicycles, he got a job as a travelling salesman for the Persil Flexible Wheel Tyre Syndicate. His job here included setting up a branch in Dublin, and he seems to have become such a successful salesman that he soon left Persil's and took up the challenge of selling bicycles for the Coventry cycle maker of Starley Brothers. Here he increased the number

1901 Johnson, fitted with the oldest known J.A.P. engine. Now on display at the Farming Museum at Normanby Hall near Scunthorpe.

of wholesale customers from 5 to 200, during his four year stay. So with a wealth of experience in the trade, 1890 saw George leave Starley's to set up his own business, in Home Street, Scunthorpe, selling bicycles and accessories. By 1896 he had moved to premises in Stafford Street and High Street, and began the manufacture of bicycles, before again returning to premises in Home Street. The bicycles manufactured were sold as Britannia, this being the base model, St Oswald, for racing cycles, the Johnson, the mid range machine, and the Royal Johnson being the top of the range machine selling for 16 Guineas cash in 1899! Upon returning to Home Street, George had changed the company name to the Beeston Cycle and Motor Works. As a measure of the company's success over the years, at the start it occupied approximately 20 square yards of space, but by 1899 this had grown to over 500 square yards! George was especially proud of his factory's 'elastic process' enamelling facility, which was meant to allow the enamel to remain undamaged even if struck by a hammer! They had also invested in the very best of American designed lathes, which according to one contemporary observer could do virtually anything, including turn, cut screws, drill, slide and surface!

1901 saw the production of the first Johnson motorcycles. These were fitted with a 1¾ horsepower Minerva engine, a trembler coil and surface carburettor. 1903 saw the introduction of a 2 hp unit, together with mechanical valves and a spray carburettor. An advertisement from The Motor of March the 4th 1903, states the 2 hp machine was available with either Dunlop or Clipper tyres, B.S.A. or Chater Lea fittings, rim brake, 'British' belt and all accessories for 35 Guineas cash with a 12 month guarantee. I must point out that the 'British' belt was actually a make of belt, and does not just disclose the country of it's manufacture. It was advertised at the time as being the only belt that could stand up to the powerful new 2¾ hp engines!

The 2hp Minerva engine was not offered for long, as Johnson soon swapped over to a 2½ hp J.A.P. engine. Again this used a surface carburettor and was fitted with a J.A.P Adjustable Spark gap. This ingenious little device allowed the rider to alter the ignition timing from the riding position, and therefore the performance of the engine. It is not known how many motorcycles were made, but we do know manufacture of cycles and motorcycles ceased in 1905. George Johnson then carried on in bicycle sales and repair until his recorded bankruptcy in 1913.

The machine depicted here is the only know survivor, frame number 107, made in 1901. We believe Johnson started the motorcycle frame numbers at 100, as was common, so this is probably motorcycle number 7. It was discovered in 1956 on the second floor of a cobbler's shop in the lower part of Scunthorpe High Street, which was owned at the time by George Johnson's brother Ben. After restoration at the time, by Ted Steeper of Broughton, it was rallied for many years, and due to it's surface carburettor had to be run either on watch cleaning solvent or lighter fluid!

Although made in 1901, this bike was not registered until 1904, which suggests it was George Johnson's demonstrator/experimental machine. We know it was originally fitted with a Minerva engine, but was fitted with a 2½ hp JAP engine when sold. From it's log book, the machine was first registered on the 7th of April 1904 to a Mr William Sewell of High Street, Ashby, as a 2½hp Johnson weighing 112 pounds. Incidentally, with a serial number of 308, this Johnson is fitted with the earliest JAP engine known to survive.

The machine is now in the care of North Lincolnshire Council, having been purchased by them with funding provided by the Science Museum PRISUM fund and the Friends of Scunthorpe Museums. It has been completely restored to running order and is now on display in the Farming Museum at Normanby Hall Country Park, near Scunthorpe.

The Johnson works in Scunthorpe c1900 (North Lincolnshire Museum)

Kirby & Edwards Ltd, Lincoln

See Lincoln Elk

Kendall, Grantham

Kendall Productions Ltd only ran for one year from 1945 to 46. William Dennis Kendall was the Independent Member of Parliament for Grantham from 1942 until 1950. He had set up a factory called the British Manufacture & Research Co Ltd during the second world war to make munitions. Before the war ended it would produce over 52 million rounds of ammunition! In 1944, with the end of hostilities in sight, Kendall announced the aim of providing large scale employment for members of his constituency after the war, by switching his company from the manufacture of arms to that of transport for the masses. He intended to build a true 'peoples car'.

This first car produced was a two door saloon fitted with a rear mounted 700cc three cylinder radial engine, which had been designed by a Horace Beaumont. The car was so basic it lacked a synchromesh gearbox or electric starter and only had one headlight. In trials the vehicle proved far from satisfactory. For example in August 1945 William Kendall arranged to drive one from the factory to London, in order to demonstrate it to fellow MPs. However such was the unreliability of the car that it is certain that it went on a trailer. A factory engineer even doubted that it was capable of travelling the last mile from Whitehall to Parliament Square under it's own power, let alone all the way from Grantham! As a result of this disaster Horace Beaumont was fired. As an aside Beaumont was later jailed for a fraud involving an electric car design.

Kendall moved quickly to resolve the disaster, and a completely new design was launched with a full width body, and a re-designed engine. Unfortunately this did not perform much better than the original, so the engine was quickly replaced with a Volkswagen unit. Although this engine improved performance and reliability, it so embarrassed Kendall that whenever the car was shown to the public the engine cover was locked!

Gregoire designed Kendall. (Michael Worthington-Williams)

So with a disastrous track record of in-house car design Kendall decided to buy in a car design from elsewhere. The design chosen came from a French company called A.F.G, which stood for Aluminium-Francaise-Gregoire. The design was penned by a Paris born engineer named Jean Albert Gregoire. As well as an engineer and vehicle builder Jean was an extremely talented individual as he was also a writer, athlete, racing driver and inventor. A pioneer of front wheel drive in the 1920's, he had turned his attention to lightweight aluminium designs, first seen in a French Amilcar of 1938. The version produced by Kendall had an air cooled flat twin engine of 594cc, driving the front wheels, and a two door saloon body with roll-back canvas roof, similar to the Citroen 2CV. Kendall built five of these cars, plus one open roadster version before his backers withdrew their support. This was at least partly due to Kendall's decision to sell his cars through the Co-operative Wholesale Society, instead of the usual Society of Motor Manufacturers and Traders. The company closed in November 1946.

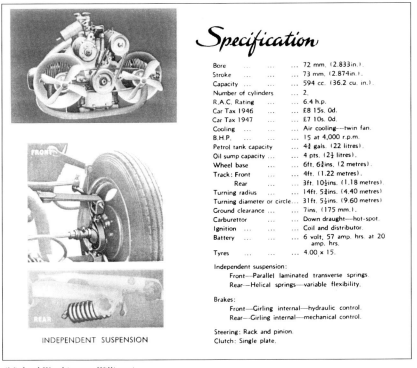

Specification

Bore	... 72 mm. (2.833in.).
Stroke	... 73 mm. (2.874in.).
Capacity	... 594 cc. (36.2 cu. in.).
Number of cylinders	... 2.
R.A.C. Rating ...	... 6.4 h.p.
Car Tax 1946 ...	... £8 15s. 0d.
Car Tax 1947 ...	... £7 10s. 0d.
Cooling	... Air cooling—twin fan.
B.H.P.	... 15 at 4,000 r.p.m.
Petrol tank capacity	... 4¼ gals. (22 litres).
Oil sump capacity ...	... 4 pts. (2½ litres).
Wheel base ...	... 6ft. 6¾ins. (2 metres).
Track: Front ...	... 4ft. (1.22 metres).
Rear ...	... 3ft. 10½ins. (1.18 metres).
Turning radius ...	... 14ft. 5⅜ins. (4.40 metres)
Turning diameter or circle...	31ft. 5⅜ins. (9.60 metres)
Ground clearance ...	... 7ins. (175 mm.).
Carburettor ...	... Down draught—hot-spot.
Ignition	... Coil and distributor.
Battery	... 6 volt, 57 amp. hrs. at 20 amp. hrs.
Tyres	... 4.00 x 15.

Independent suspension:
  Front—Parallel laminated transverse springs.
  Rear—Helical springs—variable flexibility.

Brakes:
  Front—Girling internal—hydraulic control.
  Rear—Girling internal—mechanical control.

Steering: Rack and pinion.
Clutch: Single plate.

INDEPENDENT SUSPENSION

(Michael Worthington-Williams)

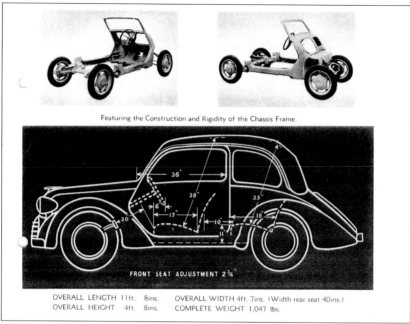

Kendall chassis frame (Michael Worthington-Williams)

It should also be noted that the between 1945 and 1946 the company also experimented by making a number of small tractors, suitable for market gardeners etc.

William Kendall eventually moved to the United States, where he had previously worked before the war, this time becoming involved with outboard motor designs for boats and electrical devices for treating arthritis.

The Gregoire design was continued by Hartnett of Melbourne, Australia, who purchased the remains of the Kendall project, and the design also formed the basis of a new Panhard car in France.

Lincoln-Elk, Lincoln

The company of Kirby and Edwards started in 1891 as bicycle manufacturers. The machines they produced soon gained a reputation for being well made, light in weight and competitively priced, and the company prospered. Their three storey showroom and factory premises

44

were at 4-5 Broadgate in Lincoln, on the site of the present telephone exchange.

The first Lincoln Elk motorcycle appeared in 1902. Also at about this time Mr Edwards left the company, leaving James Kirby as sole proprietor.

The first motorcycle made was a 2¼hp single cylinder machine. The frame was based on bicycle practice, with a loop running below the engine crankcase and an extra crossbar below the fuel tank. The fuel tank also had a separate oil tank incorporated, and also housed the accumulator for the De Dion type ignition system, behind a hinged flap. Throttle control was via a lever on the right hand side of the tank. Power to the rear wheel was via a vee section belt, and stirrup bicycle type brakes were fitted to both wheels. A bicycle type crank and pedals was used connected to the rear hub via a chain to start the engine and also to give the optimistically titled 'light pedal assistance' on steep hills.

c1908 Lincoln-Elk. Note frame tube below crankcase. (Ray Meggett)

The same basic machine was still being offered in 1908, but by now power output had grown to 3hp. Using a 7/8" Stanley-Dermatine belt, Palmer tyres on 26" rims and a Brown and Barlow carburettor it had a claimed top speed of 40 miles per hour. The basic price of this machine was £19 10 s. One of these machines, ridden by a Mr Buxton, won a bronze medal on the 1908 London to Edinburgh run.

About this time mention was made in the automotive press that the company had manufactured a car. However no details have been forthcoming and it would appear to just be a prototype that went no further. The firm did try their hand at other things occasionally, and even made a children's fairground ride at one time!

By 1910 the company were offering three new models, all using a newly designed low frame. These were all single cylinder four stroke machines, and were named model A, B and C. The lightweight Model C had a power output of 2¼hp and sold for £28 10s, while the large 3½hp Model A was yours for £34 or £37 if fitted with a Mabon free engine clutch. The most popular model was the 3hp Model B which was advertised as being fitted with Druid spring forks, handlebar controlled Brown and Barlow carburettor, footrests, carrier and stand. All models now used Bosch magneto ignition and had pannier tool bags mounted on the rear carriers. The performance and reliability of these new machines must have been good because a Mr J R Brown is recorded as winning a gold medal in the 1910 'London to Exeter and Back' trial on a Model A! The following year he took another gold on the London to Edinburgh run!

In 1911 an important innovation was offered by the factory in the form of a patented two speed gear for the two larger models. The gearing was carried on a separate shaft and operated by external expanding clutches. In high gear the drive went from the engine to the countershaft by a chain and then to the rear wheel via the drive belt. In low gear the belt ran free and the drive to the wheel is transmitted entirely by chain. The price for a Model A with two speed gearing and free engine clutch was £42 but if you didn't want either the clutch or gears, a base model fixed gear Model A came in at £34.

In 1913 the Model C had it's power increased to 2¾hp and the company added two new models to the range. The first new model was the Model S which was a 597cc, 4½hp single with two speed gearing as standard. Doing away with pedal starting, this machine also had a kick starter! Aluminium footboards were also fitted. It was advertised as being particularly suitable for sidecar work, and had a list price of £46.

"Lincoln Elk" 1912 $3\frac{1}{2}$ H.P. Model A.

Straight or Sloping Frame as desired.

SPECIFICATION.   **Total weight 160 lb.**

ENGINE. Lincoln Elk, special design of great flexibility, 85 x 88 mm., heavy flywheels, hard phosphor bronze to all bearings, mechanically operated valves of large diameter and interchangeable, strong half-time gear wheels, each valve operated by its own cam with independent rockers.

IGNITION. Bosch 1912 magneto, chain driven, in aluminium case.

CARBURETTOR. Brown and Barlow 1912, with variable Jet.

CONTROL. Entirely handle-bar control.

TRANSMISSION. By $\frac{7}{8}''$ Shamrock belt. **GEAR.** $4\frac{1}{4}$ to 1 or as ordered.

FRAME. Strong graceful design, with Druid spring forks. Wheelbase 53". Special cradle and bracket in which engine is carried by four bolts only. Height to top of saddle 32".

BRAKES. Bowden front rim brake applied from handlebar, and belt rim brake operated by simple pedal on footrests.

WHEELS. 26" carrying $2\frac{1}{4}''$ Palmer motor-cycle tyres.

TANK. Petrol capacity $1\frac{1}{2}$ gallons (this machine runs 80 to 100 miles to the gallon), lubricating oil for 400 miles, fed by force pump on tank.

SADDLE. Brooks' " B 130 " large size, with buffer springs.

STAND. Swing, easily let down, very steady.

FOOTRESTS. Special, with comfortable rubber pads.

CARRIER. Special tubular, carried in strong clips, easily detached. Toolbag

PRICE (as per above specification) **£34.**

Enamelled Brown, 10/- extra.

" **LINCOLN ELK.**" Countershaft, 2-speed gear and free engine, £8 extra.
,,   ,,   Free Engine, Clutch, £2 10s. 0d. extra.
,,   ,,   Variable pulley, 10s. 0d. extra.

"Lincoln Elk" 1912 3 H.P.   Model B.

Straight or Sloping Frame as desired.

SPECIFICATION.   **Total weight 150 lb.**

ENGINE. Lincoln Elk, very flexible. Special design, 79 x 82 mm. Hard phosphor bronze to all bearings. M.O. valves, interchangeable, large diameter, each operated from its own cam with independent rocker, strong half-time wheels.

IGNITION. Bosch 1912 magneto, chain driven, in aluminium case.

CARBURETTOR. Brown and Barlow 1912, with variable Jet.

CONTROL. Entirely handle-bar control.

TRANSMISSION. Shamrock-Gloria, ⅞" belt.   **GEAR.** 5 to 1 or as ordered.

FRAME. Strong graceful design, Druid spring forks, Wheelbase 53". Special cradle and bracket in which engine is carried by four bolts only. Height to top of saddle 32".

BRAKES. Bowden front rim brake with lever on handlebar, and belt rim brake operated by simple pedal on footrests.

WHEELS. 26" with 2" Palmer motor-cycle tyres.

TANK. Petrol tank holds 1½ gallons (this model runs 80 to 120 miles to the gallon), lubricating capacity for 400 miles, fed by force pump on tank.

SADDLE. Brooks' " B 130," large size, very comfortable, with buffer springs.

STAND. Swing, easily let down, very steady.

FOOTRESTS. Special, with comfortable rubber pads.

CARRIER. Special tubular, carried in strong clips, easily detached. Toolbag.

PRICE (as per above specification) **£30 10s.**

Enamelled Brown, 10/- extra.

" **LINCOLN ELK**," Countershaft, 2-speed gear and free engine, £8 extra.
     ,,   ,,   Free Engine Clutch, £2 10s. 0d. extra.
     ,,   ,,   Variable pulley, 10s. 0d. extra.

48

"Lincoln Elk" 1912 Lightweight 2¼ H.P. Model C.

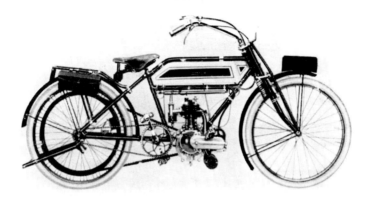

Straight or Sloping Frame as desired.

SPECIFICATION.   **Total weight 120 lb.**

ENGINE.—Special light "Lincoln Elk," 70 x 72 mm., very flexible, ample flywheels. M.O.V. both valves of large diameter and interchangeable, timing gear wheels specially strong, each valve operated by its own cam and with independent rockers.

IGNITION.—Bosch 1912 magneto, chain driven, in aluminium case.

CARBURETTOR.—Brown and Barlow 1912 pattern, with variable Jet.

CONTROL.—Entirely handle-bar control.

TRANSMISSION.—Shamrock-Gloria ⅞" belt.

GEAR.—6½ to 1 as standard.

FRAME.—Graceful design, low and comfortable. Druid spring forks, Wheelbase 49½". Special cradle and bracket in which engine is carried by four bolts. Height to top of saddle 30½".

BRAKES.—Bowden front rim brake, with lever on handlebar. Belt rim brake operated by simple pedal on footrests.

WHEELS.—26", fitted with 1¾" Palmer motor-cycle tyres.

TANK.—Petrol tank holds 1½ gallons (this machine runs 120 miles to the gallon), lubrication capacity of 400 miles, fed by force pump on tank.

SADDLE.—Brooks' "B 130" with buffer springs.

STAND.—Swing.

FOOTRESTS.—Special with comfortable rubber pads.

CARRIER.—Strong tubular, and Toolbag.

PRICE (as per above specification) **£28 10s.**

Enamelled Brown, 10/- extra.

13314

49

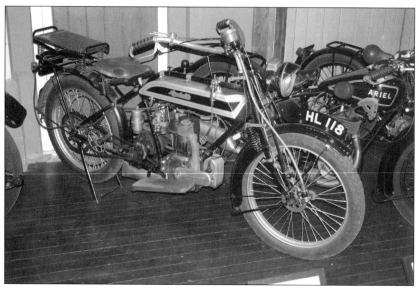

Post World War One Lincoln Elk Model B. Note kick starter!

The other new model introduced in 1913 used an identical frame setup as the 4½hp model but was fitted with a 770cc V-twin engine rated at 6hp. The list price for this machine was £55. In the 1914 London to Edinburgh run a Mr Applebee is recorded as having won a Special Gold Medal on one of these machines. 1913 also saw the company introduce two sidecar designs, one of which was considered as perfect for racing use.

In 1914 the company announced that they were developing a 2½hp two-stroke machine, and it would go on sale from the spring of 1915. However the First World War seems to have stopped it's introduction as there is no further mention of it in any company advertising. In common with other engineering companies war work was now top priority.

At the end of the war production of motorcycles was again started, but the range was slimmed down to three machines, these being the 6hp twin, now designated the Model A, the 4½hp Model B and the lightweight 2¾hp Model C.

The same range of machines continued to be manufactured over the next few years, but by 1922 Sturmey-Archer 3 speed gearboxes were specified for the two larger models, and the lightweight Model C got the two speed Lincoln Elk system.

In 1924 the company published it's catalogue for the following season. All three machines were now fitted with Sturmey-Archer 3 speed gearboxes and all had full chain drive. However 1924 was to be the company's final year.

Much was made in company advertising over the years that, except for components such as magnetos, tyres, saddles and carburettors, everything was made in the Lincoln factory. It is believed however that the company did not have a foundry, so rough castings were probably bought in and machined in house. Another legend from the factory is that all machines were tested by racing them against the clock from the factory to the top of Lindum Hill. Failure to make the required time meant re-working the engine until it did!

Quite a few Lincoln Elk machines still survive including a post war machine in the Museum of Lincolnshire Life on Burton Road in Lincoln, and a 1910 lightweight in the National Motorcycle Museum in Solihull in the West Midlands.

Lincolnshire and District Motor Body Works, Louth & Grimsby

Also known over the years as 'LL Motor Body Works', 'Thompson & Co' or just 'Lincolnshire' they were primarily a builder of bus bodies, but also built car bodies on Bentley, Daimler and Hispano-Suiza chassis'. Ceased making vehicle bodies and became a bus operator in the 1920's.

Lloyd, Grimsby

In1911 Fred Lloyd gave up life as a fish merchant and opened a garage in Lovett Street, New Cleethorpes. In 1920 he also purchased premises in Strand Street, by which time sales and service agencies were held for the car makers of Sheffield-Simplex, Star, Grimsby, Hupmobile, Itala, and Ford.

In 1922 the company bought more premises, at Nun's Farm, which became Nun's Garage. The Lovett Street garage was therefore sold and the company also became limited, registered as Fred Lloyd (Motors) Ltd.

During this period sales agencies held included Bean, Belsize, Chandler, Crossley, Galloway, Mathis, Nash, Peugeot, Salmon, Vulcan and Willis-Overland.

1922 also saw Fred's son, Roland, become the company's managing director, at the age of just eighteen. Not long after this he built a special for himself, from bits of car lying about the workshop. This experience eventually led to the design and production of a prototype car intended for production. It was to become the Lloyd 350.

Lloyd Cars Ltd was formed in 1935, and took up new premises on Patrick Street in Grimsby. Limited production started soon after. The Lloyd 350 was powered by a rear mounted water cooled Villiers 347cc two stroke engine. Drive was transmitted via a chain to a three speed, plus reverse, Albion gearbox, and then via another chain, through a Hardy-Spicer universal joint to the nearside rear wheel. Engine cooling was by thermo-syphon, and rear mounted radiator. Coil ignition was used with automatic retard and advance. A horizontal lever outside the car on the offside was used as the starting handle. A detachable hood and side screens were provided, which could be folded away behind the seat. As the engine was rear mounted, there was ample legroom. In addition both the spare wheel and battery were stowed up front, under the bonnet. A full tool kit was also provided as standard, as was a hand operated windscreen wiper. The standard colour scheme was black with red mudguards, headlamps, wheels and leathercloth upholstery. The chassis used a five inch diameter, high grade tubular steel backbone with cantilever type pressed steel cross members.

A magazine at the time called The Light Car tested a 350 at Brooklands, whilst carrying two twelve stone men. It recorded a flying quarter mile at 20.1 seconds, which was a speed of 44.78 miles per hour. As well as fair performance, the price of a 350 also compared well against it's competition selling for just £80, against £100 for the likes of a Ford Popular. Additionally the fuel economy claimed by Lloyd's was 50miles per gallon!

As well as British sales, export orders for the 350 were also taken from Australia, Holland and South Africa.

Lloyd 350 side view. Note pull-start handle on sill! (Michael Worthington-Williams)

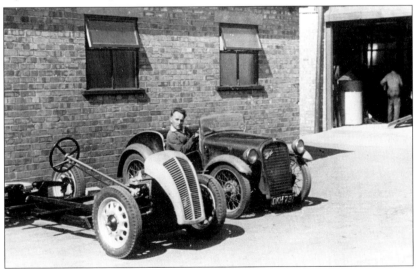

A 1946 Lloyd rolling chassis and a 1937 Lloyd 350 (National Motor Museum)

Considerable publicity was gained for Lloyd in 1938 when a fleet of ten 350's were purchased by The Gas Light & Coke Company for use by their inspectors. All were painted dark green, with the company lettering in gold.

In 1939 a 5cwt van version of the 350 was introduced, at a price of £95 in primer or £98 if painted in blue or green. Mechanically it was the same as the car but it was fitted with pressed steel wheels and had a front mounted engine driving the front wheels. Very few were produced before war halted production in 1939. As with most other automotive companies at the time Lloyd's soon ceased car production and took up war contracts. These included the production of parts for Spitfire and Hurricane airframes, and the manufacture of components for Rolls-Royce Merlin engines. These war contracts proved lucrative for Lloyd, not only in financial terms, but also in obtaining modern manufacturing machinery and skilled staff.

With the end of hostilities the company quickly built on developments made before the war and introduced the 650 car in 1946. The company had experimented in 1939 by fitting the 347cc Villiers engine from the 350 with cylinders of their own design, in order to aid cooling. These experiments went a stage further in 1945/6, when Lloyd announced a two stroke, twin cylinder engine of their own design and manufacture. With a capacity of 645cc, it was mounted transversally at the front of a new design of car and chassis. The cylinders were of aluminium alloy, with iron liners and the fuel was delivered to the engine by the new Lloyd patented charging pump. This new car drove the front wheels using the same basic layout as the pre-war 350 vans, and transmitted the power via twin shafts through an all synchromesh, four speed gearbox. A double backbone chassis was used, as was independent suspension all round with coil springs. The company prided itself on making almost all the components for it's cars, and as well as the chassis, body and engine, Lloyd even made the wheels and brakes! Power output was quoted as 25bhp, and a contemporary magazine test in 1950 recorded 42mpg at a steady 40mph.

The 650 went on sale proper in 1948, but at £480 it was poor value compared to it's competitors, such as the 918cc Morris Series E convertible which sold for just £346. However, due to the early post war government order of 'export or die', cars for the home market were in extremely short supply. This meant that, poor value or not, Lloyd still had trouble keeping up with demand! Export orders also arrived from all over the world, even America, and plans were made to add to the range, by introducing both a saloon car and a van. But with design problems to be sorted out and materials shortages, output never bettered five cars per week.

Whichever way you look at it...
A SOUND JOB

The clean symmetrical lines and handsome appearance of the LLOYD "650" will be instantly appreciated. As an open tourer it is particularly pleasing to note that the hood is completely concealed behind the rear seat squab whilst the hood and sidescreens are so designed that when erected the protection offered is equal to the average drop-head coupe. Comfort is obvious at a glance and appeal is further sharpened by almost unbelievable thrift—the result of the adaption of advanced engineering principles.

Lloyd 650 (Michael Worthington-Williams)

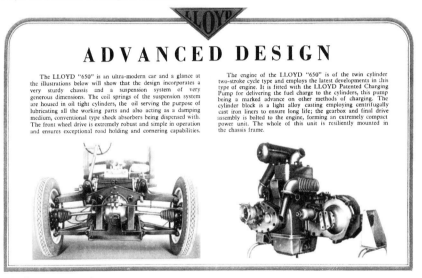

ADVANCED DESIGN

The LLOYD "650" is an ultra-modern car and a glance at the illustrations below will show that the design incorporates a very sturdy chassis and a suspension system of very generous dimensions. The coil springs of the suspension system are housed in oil tight cylinders, the oil serving the purpose of lubricating all the working parts and also acting as a damping medium, conventional type shock absorbers being dispensed with. The front wheel drive is extremely robust and simple in operation and ensures exceptional road holding and cornering capabilities.

The engine of the LLOYD "650" is of the twin cylinder two-stroke cycle type and employs the latest developments in this type of engine. It is fitted with the LLOYD Patented Charging Pump for delivering the fuel charge to the cylinders, this pump being a marked advance on other methods of charging. The cylinder block is a light alloy casting employing centrifugally cast iron liners to ensure long life; the gearbox and final drive assembly is bolted to the engine, forming an extremely compact power unit. The whole of this unit is resiliently mounted in the chassis frame.

Lloyd 650 engine and suspension
(Michael Worthington-Williams)

Unfortunately the end of car production came in 1951, when more orthodox and cheaper vehicles from bigger manufacturers became more readily available. The company continued as general engineers, producing components for Rolls-Royce, Aston Martin, Lotus and others, and finally closed in 1983. Car production has been estimated at around 150 pre-war 350's and approximately 400 of the post war model.

Marshall, Gainsborough

The company of P.F.E. Marshall was in existence for only one year from 1919 until 1920, and made a small number of cars fitted with Coventry-Simplex F type engines. Although of the same name and in the same town, there was no connection between this obscure make of car and the famous engineering company of Marshall, Sons & Co Ltd.

National and Rose National, Gainsborough

The engineering company of Rose Brothers was founded in 1895, specialising in making machinery to pack cigarettes and chocolates. In fact Cadbury's famous 'Roses' chocolates are named after the maker of the machinery that originally wrapped them!

In 1902 the company decided to expand into car manufacture, and in that year announced two models. These cars were powered by engines of two cylinder 10/12 horsepower and three cylinder 20/24 horsepower respectively. Both models featured shaft drive and were designed by Edward and Frank Baines (see Baines Ltd). In 1905 a four cylinder 20/24hp model was introduced. However there is conjecture over the next model announced, with six cylinders, as no evidence exists that it was ever even made as a prototype, let alone a production car.

It is believed that car production ceased in 1906, although an early motoring book called The Automobile, written by Paul Hasluck, claimed that National were making three cylinder 18/22hp cars and 24 to 40hp four cylinder versions as late as 1909. Rose Brothers publicity claimed an even later date of 1912. And to make the confusion even greater there was another National car made in Manchester from 1904 until about 1906. It would appear however that this National was a tri-car.

Whatever is the truth, the Lincolnshire made National, sometimes called Rose National, are known to have made both the engine and chassis for their vehicles, with bodies being made for them by outside contractors, most notably Hamshaw of Leicester. It is believed that no more than fifty cars were produced, most of them being the 18/22hp three cylinder model.

1906 National 20/24hp tourer (National Motor Museum)

Engine from a Rose National car on display at the Museum of Lincolnshire Life. Reputed to have been fitted to a Brooklands racing car, this engine survived as it was later fitted to the Rose Bros works fire engine!

Pick and New Pick, Stamford

John Henry Pick, better known as Jack, was born in 1867 in Stamford, to Robert and Catherine Pick. Robert was the publican of the Welland Cottage Inn, and also a butcher. Upon completing his education at the age of thirteen, Jack began work at a brickworks in Stamford. However he did not stay long, and soon went to work at a grocer's shop as an errand boy. At the age of sixteen he moved again and became an apprentice to a blacksmith in Little Bytham, just north of Stamford. Here he learned the basics of engineering.

In 1887 he took a job in Stamford at the blacksmiths shop of George Jefferies and Edward Blackstone, and within eighteen months had risen to be foreman blacksmith.

However in the early 1890's he left to work for the Harrison Patents Company, which had been set up to exploit engineering and agricultural patents. Here he patented his first design, in partnership with a Thomas Fountain, for a new type of weed hoe. Another patent followed, also for gardening tools, but 1894 saw him returning briefly to Blackstone's, to help solve a problem with a rotary digging machine, before he set up on his own in 1895, in order to manufacture his patent hoes.

In 1896 Pick decided to enter the rapidly expanding bicycle trade, and set up as a cycle dealer at 5 Blackfriars Street, Stamford, in partnership with a local iron merchant by the name of Anthony Pledger. However his partner soon moved on, leaving Pick to run the company alone. Trading as J. H. Pick & Co, he continued repairing and selling bicycles and also making his patent hoes and, of all things, rug needles! The business prospered and by 1899 was employing forty men, and the premises were expanded. By this time they were advertising bicycles made to special order within four days!

1899 was also the year Pick decided to build his first car. Using an unspecified French made petrol engine, the result was a tiller steered four wheel 'dog cart', and was sold to a Dr Benson of Market Deeping for the princely sum of £85!

1900 brought more sales, and Pick also developed, and successfully patented, a new form of front suspension. This involved both front wheels being fitted into bicycle type forks with each fork turning in it's own headstock. These headstocks were joined together with a cross tube. Curved leaf springs fastened between the two headstocks and the tubular steel chassis. This allowed a small amount of independent suspension travel for each wheel.

Jack Pick driving the two seater in 1900. The location is Priory Road in Stamford. Note the patented front fork steering setup. (Photo Stamford Museum)

Later in 1900 Pick exhibited two cars at the Stanley Cycle Show in London. The first was a four seat dog cart fitted with a water cooled, single cylinder de Dion engine of 4½hp. The power was transmitted directly to the rear axle via two friction clutches. Two gears were provided. The second car was a two seat voiturette, powered by an air cooled engine of 2¾hp. Power transmission, again with two speeds, was the same as on the dog cart. In both cases a top speed of 25mph was claimed, and each car was fitted with a foot operated band brake and a hand brake which operated by pressing a paddle directly onto the offside rear tyre.

In March 1900 the Pick Motor Company Ltd was formed. Financial backing was to be provided by a group of new directors. These were Sir George Whitcote Bt, W. Bean, the Reverend Tryon and an iron founder named Charles Gray. The chairman appointed was the Marquis of Exeter. Surprisingly Pick was not appointed as a director, but instead was given the position of works manager. This meant he had no say in the running of the company or any sales decisions. What really annoyed him however, was that he was also overruled on engineering matters, even though only one director, Charles Gray, had any form of mechanical knowledge. One such decision which the board took was over the choice of car engines and another, which really caused conflict, was their decision to sell off the successful cycle making side of the business in March 1902.

1901 saw new engines of 3½hp for the voiturette, and 6hp water cooled twin for the dog cart. However the real advances did not come until 1902 when the company announced production of it's own engines. Against Jack Pick's advice, the board had decided upon developing two horizontally opposed, water cooled twins, developing 6hp and 10hp respectively. The engines were fitted transversally at the front of the car, with the radiator in front. Drive was via two cross belts driven from two different sized pulleys mounted on the end of the crankshaft. These belts drove free and fixed pulleys on a countershaft, which was mounted behind the rear axle. A sliding clutch on this countershaft between the two pulleys (one high speed and one low speed) engaged a sprocket which drove a chain which was connected to the differential on the rear axle. Another advance at this time was the fitting of a steering wheel as opposed to the usual tiller! Prices were quoted as £130 for the 4hp car, raising to £150 for the 6hp model. The single cylinder voiturette was also still available, but was now of 4hp.

Jack and Walter Pick in a 1901/2 Pick Voiturette. (Photo Stamford Museum)

The following year, 1903, Pick took two stands at the Crystal Palace Motor Show, in order to display three 6hp two seater cars, one 10hp two seater, four 10hp Tonneaus (of differing designs) and a working model of Pick's new patent cam operated band brake! In addition a 6hp Voiturette and a 10hp Tonneau car were doing demonstration runs in the grounds! Apart from the new braking system, which operated on the rear wheels only, another innovation was the launch of two new chain drive cars, using the 6hp and 10hp engine respectively. Drive was via a clutch shaft on the end of the crank, driving a Panhard type gearbox using a Reynold's chain. The gearbox had three forward speeds, plus reverse, and drove the back axle using a chain. The price of a standard 10hp four seater was now advertised at £270.

It should come as no surprise that, with such an expanding range of vehicles, 1903 saw the factory again being expanded, on a two acre site between St Leonard's Street and Blackfriars Street. New machinery was installed which allowed the company to produce almost all their own components, including gearboxes, engines, chassis', bodies and upholstery. Sales agencies had also been opened in London and Dublin.

A 1903 photo of the Pick works in Gas Lane Stamford. (Photo Stamford Museum)

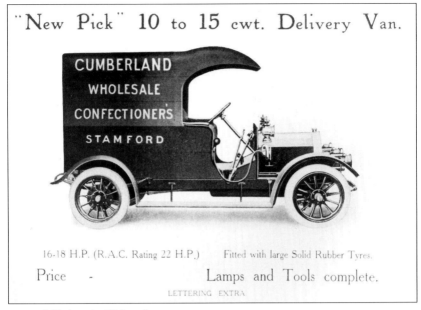

Van available from the 1910 catalogue.

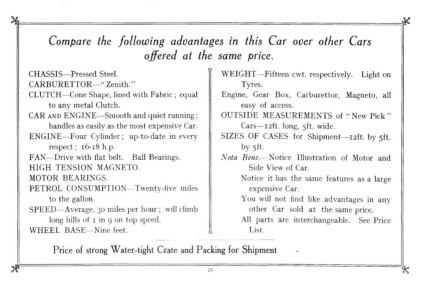

But despite all this optimism, 1903 was to see the problems between Jack Pick and the board come to a head. The company had entered two cars for the Royal Automobile Club's 1000 mile reliability trial, which the board decided to withdraw. Jack was so annoyed he took a four seater on a reliability trail of his own, where it proved trouble free. However on returning to work he was suspended by the board for his actions.

What happened next at the company is not clear. It exhibited cars at the Crystal Palace Motor Show in February 1904, but by September adverts were placed in various newspapers in order to try to sell the works. Jack himself was no longer with them, and had left to set up the new company of J.H. Pick & Co at 11 High Street, St Martin's, with former Pick director Charles Gray as his partner.

The Pick Motor Company was by now under new management and all car production had ceased. The company changed it's name to the Blackfriars Motor and Engineering Works and took a sales agency for the American made Orient Buckboard. It was not a success and the company was wound up in 1906.

Shortly after leaving the Pick Motor Company, Jack started in business again under his old company name of J.H. Pick & Co, at premises at 11 High Street, Stamford. His capital amounted to £285 plus a £100 loan from former Pick director Charles Gray. As a measure of Jack's popularity, several ex-Pick employees so came to work for him. Initially, just to keep afloat, the company took on any light engineering work that came their way and they also sold petrol and tyres. While this kept his employee's occupied, Jack was busy working on a new design of chassis and engine, the first of which was completed in 1906. This new car was fitted with a two seat body built by the Stamford company of Hayes and Son. The engine was a vertical four cylinder unit, rated at 12-14hp. Each of the four cylinders was an individual casting, and had opposing inlet and exhaust valves. Power transmission was via a cone clutch, two speed gearbox and propeller shaft to a live rear axle. A foot pedal operated a transmission brake on the propeller shaft, and the two rear drum brakes were operated by the handbrake.

Just before announcing this new car, the company was re-named the New Pick Motor Company. Additional premises were also acquired from Pick's body suppliers of Hayes and Son. These were situated on the corner of High Street, St Martins and Barnack Road. Hayes and Son continued production at their other premises on Scotgate.

By 1908 the cars had been developed further and the engines were now rated at 14-16hp, by increasing the bore to 90mm and the stroke to 103mm. They were also fitted with high tension magnetos and all cars now had three speed gearboxes. By 1910 the company was advertising seven different models with the basic two seater costing 170 Guineas and the four seater 195 Guineas. A racing version was also available at 170 Guineas and had a claimed top speed of fifty miles per hour! If you wanted to build your own body a rolling chassis was also available at 144 Guineas. The wheelbase of all the cars was nine feet.

In 1911 the big change was to the engine, when the previously specified four individual cast cylinders with opposed valves were replaced by a single casting with valves all on one side of the engine driven by a single camshaft. The stroke was also increased to 127mm giving an increase in power from 12-14hp to 16-18hp. This was followed in 1912 by a new range of vehicles, all fitted with the new monobloc engine. As well as the usual standard model two and four seaters, Pick also introduced the sporty looking 'Torpedo' models. Available with either two seats (with or without Dicky seat) or four, the main styling difference was a round radiator grille and barrel shaped bonnet. Advertising at the time stressed the novelty of all the control levers now being inside the car! A heavy duty chassis was also introduced for use on two other new models, a Landaulette/Taxi and a 10 to 15cwt van. The van was fitted with solid rubber tyres. Car production continued until mid 1915 when then works was turned over to war work.

At the end of the war Pick decided not to return to car production for the time being, and instead concentrated on developing a new design of three wheeled tractor, for which a patent had been applied in August 1918. Unfortunately this very unorthodox design of tractor was a complete failure, so Pick tried a more conventional design. However this design seems to have been no more successful, and so in 1923 Pick decided to re-finance his company and entered into partnership with a local timber merchant called Charles Miles. The company was re-registered as the Pick Motor Company Limited.

Four new cars were announced for 1924, all fitted with an uprated version of the pre-war monobloc engine. By keeping the stroke at 127mm but increasing the bore to 95mm power was now up to 22½hp. The models

The PICK Sporting Model.

The 1924 Sporting Model (22.5 h.p.)

Price - £365

EQUIPMENT:

Smith's or Lucas' Self-Starter and Dynamo.

Head, Side, Tail Lamps and Electric Horn.

Aluminium Instrument Board,

beautifully finished and fully equipped with

Smith's Clock and Speedometer.

Bluemel's 18in. Steering Wheel.

5 Wheels (fitted with 765×105 Best Dunlop Cord Tyres.)

A Full Equipment of Tools with Enots Grease Gun.

Length—10 ft.   Wheel Base—4 ft. 7 in.   Track—13 ft. 8 in. over all.

THE COACH WORK.—Two Seater Sports Model Body is designed on novel and comfortable lines, with strength; the seating being low guarantees the passengers being protected from wind and weather by the scuttle dash. The skeleton is made of prime seasoned English ash, the panels are heavy gauge aluminium, which guarantees no rusting to raise the paint, also lightness, a feature that should not be *overlooked*. Upholstering of the best quality and finish, with a neat one man hood. Notice the shape of the mudguards and height of foot boards ; saving ground friction means increased speed, less Petrol consumption, with less dust, splashes, and suction on car.

Stamford Museum

available were an open two seat sporting model at £365, an open four seater for £385, a coupe at £410 and a saloon model known as the Pullman at £450. The bodies, which were available either painted or polished bare metal, were made of heavy gauge aluminium on an English ash frame. An attempt at aerodynamics was also made for the saloon and coupe models with a v-shaped radiator and rear coachwork, in order, as Pick's brochure put it, 'to save wind resistance and suction'! The cars were well appointed being fitted with either Smith's or Lucas self-starters and dynamos, electric lighting and horn, speedometer, clock, Dunlop Best Cord tyres, and carrying a full tool kit complete with an Enots grease gun! The saloon was particularly well upholstered with high grade Bedford cord for the seats and bottom quarters, smooth cloth to roof and top quarters and lace and curtains to match!

Contemporary advertising also made much of the Pick Patent Perfect Seats fitted to all models except the sporting. These seats were advertised as being movable and could be taken out of the car in five minutes to provide sleeping accommodation or to carry luggage. The factory claimed a top speed of sixty miles per hour and a typical miles per gallon figure of thirty.

However despite all this the car did not sell. It was very old fashioned in both it's performance and styling. In addition the post-war boom was coming to an end and manufacturers struggled to find business. The trend now, helped by the £1 per horsepower road tax just introduced, was for smaller cars like the Austin Seven and Morris Minor. In January 1925 the Pick Motor Company Limited went into voluntary liquidation.

John 'Jack' Pick kept possession of 11 St Martin's and set up a greengrocer's shop. At the rear of the premises he set up a small workshop where he did small engineering jobs and designed agricultural equipment. He died in 1954 aged 87.

Six complete Pick cars still exist. These are a 1901 Voiturette and a 1912 Doctors Coupe, both in Great Britain. The other four, all from the period 1912 to 1914, are in New Zealand. In addition there are three more known which are in an incomplete or derelict state. Two of these are in New Zealand and there are also the remains of a 1905 chain driven model in Australia.

Pilbeam Racing Designs, Bourne

Pilbeam Racing Designs was set up by Mike Pilbeam in the town of Bourne in 1975. Prior to this Mike had pursued a career in Formula 1 which included working for Surtees and Lotus and culminated with the post of Chief Designer for BRM. Since 1975 the company has been involved with engine, suspension and chassis development work on all kinds of motorsport projects, including Formula 1, 2, 3 and 4, rallying, saloon car racing and even motorcycle sidecar racing. Projects done for others include design and development work for Vauxhall of the Nova, Vectra, Cavalier and Calibra rally cars, Astra and Cavalier touring cars and Calibra Thundersaloon. They have also designed motorsport components for Ford, Honda, Peugeot and Hyundai cars and a new suspension system for the Lotus Elise.

However, the main focus of the company since the start has been the design and manufacture of single seat hillclimb cars. They have become so successful in this sport that, since 1977, Pilbeam designs have won the British Hillclimb Championship 17 times and also the 2003 Northern Ireland Sprint Championship!

The 1977 championship was won by chassis number MP22, which was based on a modified Brabham BT38. The engine fitted was a V8 Cosworth DFV.

With constant improvements to the designs over the years many different engines have been fitted including Hart, Brabham Repco, Judd and Toyota. Their work developing the Vauxhall 2 litre engine for touring car racing led to this engine also being specified in the MP62 single seat hillclimb car.

In 1998 the company decided to re-enter mainstream circuit racing, when work began on the MP84 project to produce a sports racing car for the International Sports Racing Series/Sports Racing World Cup. This new car made it's first competitive appearance at Spa Francochamps in May 1999 and the first production car won Round 5 of the ISRS at Donington in July of that year. This achievement is all the more notable as the car had only been finished two days before the race!

The MP84 featured a chassis made from aluminium honeycomb panels with integral stiffeners and doublers and carbon fibre body panels. Double wishbone suspension with anti-dive geometry, adjustable anti roll bars and lightweight uprights were fitted, together with Eibach springs and dampers. The engine used was a 3 litre Nissan V6 giving approximately 350hp, driving the rear wheels through a Hewland six speed sequential gearbox and three plate sintered heavy duty clutch. As required by the regulations the design underwent a crash test at MIRA prior to production to test it's frontal impact absorption structure, and passed with flying colours. In 2002 this car was developed into the MP91, which amongst many other improvements had a 3.4 litre Nissan V6 fitted to give 530bhp.

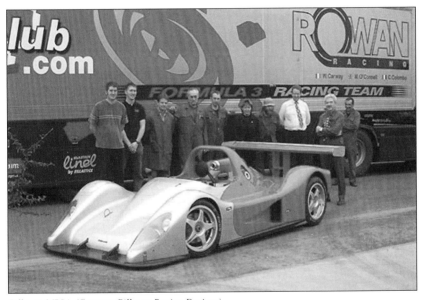

Pilbeam MP84. (Courtesy Pilbeam Racing Designs)

In 1996 the company moved to a new, purpose built factory on Graham Hill Way, a road named after the twice Formula 1 World Champion who raced for BRM. The new factory was opened by Graham's widow, Bette.

In 1999 the company turned it's attention to designing carbon fibre chassis tubs, which led to the introduction of the MP86, fitted with a Judd V8, and MP87 (Hart 4 cylinder) hillclimb cars. These in turn led to the state of the art MP88 in 2002. This has come to dominate hill climbing since it's introduction.

Pilbeam MP88 hill climb car. (Courtesy Pilbeam Racing Designs)

In 2004 the company announced it was developing a car suitable for both hill climbing and circuit racing, to be called the MP92. The first car was fitted with a 3.9 litre Cosworth DFL engine and on it's debut finished second in class, despite no development work having been carried out!

Also in 2004 the company announced it's new MP93 sports car, for the Le Mans Series. This uses a carbon fibre tub and is fitted with a JPX V6 engine. At the time of writing a new version of this car is being developed for the 2007 Le Mans Series and 24 hour race later in the year.

Raymond Mays, (Shelsley Motors Ltd) Bourne
(See also ERA and BRM)

Raymond Mays was one of the greats of British motor racing. A successful racing driver himself he was the man who, together with Humphrey Cook, founded ERA (English Racing Automobiles) before World War Two. After the war he set up BRM (British Racing Motors). The list of drivers who raced his cars reads like a Who's Who of motor racing, including Juan-Manuel Fangio, Stirling Moss and Graham Hill to name but three.

But 1938 saw him decide to change direction slightly and launch a road car, in conjunction with engineer and ERA collaborator, Peter Berthon. The company Mays set up to make the car was named Shelsley Motors Ltd after the Shelsley Walsh hill climb, where Mays had had a great deal of success in his racing career. Like the ERA, the road car was to be made in a factory behind his house. The 1939 sales brochure lists three models, these being a sports four door saloon, an open two door sports tourer, and a drophead 'foursome' Coupe. List price for all models was £495. The engine chosen was the 2868cc side valve V8 made by Standard of Coventry. It's R.A.C rating of 20hp meant the road tax for one of these cars was £15. Eighty five brake horse power was quoted and all models had independent front suspension. The claimed top speed was 90mph. Standard colours were maroon with maroon trim, grey or blue with blue trim, black with fawn trim or 'Dominion' blue with blue trim.

Raymond Mays V8 Drophead Coupe competing in the 1939 RAC Rally (National Motor Museum)

Unfortunately production ceased in 1939, due to the outbreak of the Second World War, when only five cars had been produced. Drawings still survive which show the next model to have been made was a two door saloon.

Raymond Mays himself went on to co-found BRM after the war, and also went into the garage business where he sold modified saloon cars such as

71

Ford Zephyrs. He died in 1980 and his ashes were scattered, which left no memorial to him. In 2003 this was corrected when the Bourne Motor Racing Memorial was unveiled (see separate section). In addition a road in the town of Bourne has recently been named Raymond Mays Way.

Richardson, Saxilby

Originally formed in January 1903 as the Lincoln Motor Manufacturing Company, it's name was changed in March of that year to J R Richardson & Co (Lincoln) Ltd. The managing director was Mr John R. Richardson and his fellow board members and investors were W.S. Richardson, Charles W. Pennell, H.E. Newsum, F.N. Sherwood and W.A. Cannon. Work began on the construction of the factory on Sykes Lane, Saxilby in June 1903, and, due to it's simple steel frame and corrugated iron construction, was completed in only six months. The factory was fully equipped with it's own machine tools, three pits, and an overhead crane running between the bays. The whole factory was lit by electricity and had it's own generating plant.

While the factory was being constructed the first prototype Richardson car was also being made, in Charles Pennell's packing shed in Lincoln. Premises were also acquired at Gowt's Bridge in Lincoln, at 406 High Street, for use as a showroom and workshop.

With the factory fully equipped and staffed, production began early in 1904. Three models were sold and, as was common for the day, most of the components, including the engines, were bought in from other companies. The cars produced all had open coachwork, with brakes on the rear wheels only and were available in any colour you wanted as long as it was black! However their was a choice of three engines, a 6½ horsepower single cylinder, 12 horsepower twin or an 18 horsepower four cylinder model. All these engines were purchased from the French company of Aster, who also had a manufacturing plant in Wembley, North London. The smallest model had a three speed gearbox, with four speed units fitted to the others. All cars were shaft drive. It is believed that the two smaller Richardson models offered may actually have been re-badged French made Mass cars, however we shall probably never know for sure.

1905 Richardson made in Saxilby. In the background is a Rose National made in Gainsborough. (John Wilson)

Richardson's went into liquidation in 1907, and the premises in Saxilby were bought by the engineering company of H.J. West & Co Ltd, for the manufacture of industrial refrigeration equipment. John Richardson, the company founder, stayed in the motor industry and went to work as manager for the car maker Mass at Courbevoie in France.

Rose National, Gainsborough

See National

Ruston & Hornsby, Lincoln

The company of Ruston and Hornsby Limited was formed on the 11th of September 1918 by the merger of the two famous Lincolnshire engineering firms of Ruston & Proctor Ltd and Richard Hornsby & Sons Ltd.

The origins of Ruston & Proctor can be traced back to 1840 when James Proctor and Theophilus Burton set up as millwrights and engineers in premises on Waterside South in Lincoln. On January the first 1857 they were joined by businessman Joseph Ruston. The partnership did not last long as Mr Burton became nervous of Ruston's ambitious ideas, and sold out his share of the business in July of that year for the princely sum of £855 10 shillings. And so Ruston and Proctor was born, and went on to become a very successful company manufacturing stationary and portable steam engines, railway locomotives, traction engines, threshing machines and oil engines. During the First World War they also produced A.B.C. Dragonfly aircraft engines and also set up a new factory at Boultham to construct aircraft including Sopwith Camels, Strutters and Snipes. During the war they also got involved with motor vehicles in a small way when they started manufacturing standardised pressed steel wheels and tipping bodies for lorries.

The company of Richard Hornsby & Sons Ltd goes back to 1815 when Richard Hornsby went into partnership with Richard Seaman and set up as blacksmiths and engineers in Grantham. Specialising in agricultural equipment the firm prospered. In1828 Richard Seaman retired, leaving Hornsby as sole proprietor. The firm branched out and produced items as diverse as steam engines, grass mowers, washing machines and mangles! In 1891 the company took on the manufacturing rights to a compression ignition engine invented by Herbert Akroyd Stuart. This went on sale as the Hornsby-Akroyd Patent Oil Engine. It is interesting to note that this heavy oil engine was actually on sale five years before Dr Rudolf Diesel had even constructed his first engine! Hornsby's went on to become probably the World's most important maker of stationary oil engines. One was used for many years to generate the electricity to light the Statue of Liberty in New York. Another was used by Marconi to provide the power for the World's first trans-Atlantic radio transmission. Hornsby engines also lit nearly every lighthouse in Great Britain. From 1896 Hornsby's also made a small number of oil engined tractors. In 1905 the company produced the world's first fully tracked tractor. This was named the Hornsby Chain Tractor and was powered by a 20hp Hornsby-Akroyd engine. Several other tracked vehicles were also produced including a modified French made Rochet Schneider car in 1907 and a modified Mercedes Benz the following year. Despite their excellent showing at War Department trials they were never accepted by the military, who were much to fond of horses and cavalry charges! In fact only one order for a tracked vehicle was ever received, for the famous Yukon Tractor, which used Hornsby tracks and drive and a Foster's of Lincoln steam engine and boiler. Hornsby eventually gave up on tracks in 1908 and sold all patents and rights for their tracked vehicles to the Holt Caterpillar Company in

During the First World War Ruston & Proctor made these lorry tipping bodies and pressed steel wheels. (Ray Hooley)

America. Six years later the British Army had reason to regret rejecting the tracked Hornsby machines, as the mud and trenches of France brought the First World War to a stalemate.

Towards the end of the war both companies realised that hard times lay ahead. By concentrating on war work their overseas markets were now mostly lost to them. In an effort to stay competitive after the war they decided to amalgamate and to speed this up Hornsby's went into voluntary liquidation. They were right about problems. Despite assurances by the Air Ministry that six months notice would be given before severing Ruston's war contracts, as soon as the war ended the order was given to close the Boultham works and scrap all undelivered and part built aircraft. This left the new company with the prospect of sacking several thousand workers and quite possibly destroying Lincoln's local economy at the same time.

Some of the aircraft workers were transferred to other jobs within the company, but the big problem was the large numbers of skilled woodworkers, who had been employed on aircraft production. Two courses of action were taken. Firstly to keep the workers busy and to use up the vast stocks of wood left over from aircraft production, the manufacture of furniture was started. But the main solution decided upon was to start production of cars. It is believed that Ruston's new model was influenced by an American car design available at the time fitted with a Herschell-Spillman engine.

Ruston and Hornsby car factory (Ray Hooley)

A 1920 photo showing Ruston & Hornsby cars outside the Boultham factory. (Ray Hooley)

Final preparation of Ruston & Hornsby cars in 1921. (Ray Hooley)

Superb shot of a 1921 Ruston & Hornsby rolling chassis. (Ray Hooley)

Examples of body styles from the Ruston & Hornsby 1923 catalogue.
7-Seater ¾ Landaulette. (Ray Hooley)

2-Door All Weather body. (Ray Hooley)

79

2/3 Seater body. (Ray Hooley)

Standard five seat open tourer model "Twenty" with concealed hood. (Ray Hooley)

Standard five seat open tourer model "Fifteen" with externally stowed hood and disc wheels. (Ray Hooley)

Standard five seat open tourer model "Sixteen" (Ray Hooley)

Chassis detail common for the 1923 model "Sixteen" and "Twenty". (Ray Hooley)

Model "Sixteen" with hood raised. (Ray Hooley)

81

Whatever is the basis of the design, the new model was announced in June 1919 and deliveries began in October of the same year. Designated the A1, it was powered by a 2613cc four cylinder side valve engine rated at 15.9hp. Built by Dorman's of Stafford, this engine had a bore and stroke of 80mm x 130mm and featured a detachable cylinder head, gear driven oil pump and centrifugal water pump. Drive was via an inverted cone clutch and propeller shaft to a three speed gearbox built in-unit with the rear axle. Suspension was by three quarter elliptic springs at the rear and semi-eliptics at the front. Patent Marles steering gear was fitted, and unusually for cars of this era the brake and gear levers were inside the car to the driver's left! When first announced the A1 was advertised as an open five seat tourer for £525 or as an 'all-weather' model for £575. However early production problems and material shortages did increase the price later in the 1919.

Despite being a well made and good looking car, sales in Great Britain were disappointing, due mainly to poor marketing. The company had no experience in the motor industry and so appointed C B Wardman & Co Ltd of Great Portland Street in London as sole concessionaire. Unfortunately it would appear he had too many other interests in the motor industry to promote the Ruston car fully.

Sales overseas, and particularly the Empire, were however very good. Ruston & Hornsby were well known abroad as makers of solid and dependable farm machinery and traction engines, and such a reputation helped greatly in selling the new cars to be used in tough conditions.

Two new models were added for 1920, these being the 20hp A2 and the 20/25hp A3. These two models were fitted with Ruston & Hornsby's own engine of 3308cc. The Dorman engine in the A1 was also replaced with one of identical dimensions but built in unit with the gearbox. However prices (£650 for the A1 Tourer up to £750 for the A3) were too expensive for the mass market.

Also around this time the company announced the introduction of a range of ambulances. Five different models were available, these being the Bradford, No 6 Semi 'B' type and Red Cross based on strengthened A3 car chassis' of 11 foot 6 inch wheelbase and fitted with 20/25hp engines. Two smaller versions of the Red Cross and No 6 Semi 'B' Type were also

Ruston and Hornsby Bradford Ambulance (Ray Hooley)

available which used the A1 'fifteen' chassis. Twin rear wheels were fitted as standard, but the smaller models could be specified with singles. The top of the range Bradford sold for £867 and could carry two stretchers, one above the other on the left hand side. The body used an Ash frame with Mahogany outer panels. I particularly like the fact that the Coat of Arms of the buyer could be hand painted on by the factory instead of using a transfer!

In 1921 the A2 20hp model was dropped and the A1 and A3 cars became known as 16/20 and 20/25 respectively. Prices were also dropped to £580 for the 16/20 and £650 for the larger car.

For 1923 the range was increased with the introduction of a 15hp Dorman engined model again fitted with the gearbox in unit with the rear axle. The gear change of all the models, which had been much criticized, was now much improved and the suspension on the two larger cars was now by semi-elliptic springs all round. Prices were now £476 for the 15hp, £523 for the 16hp and £575 for the 20hp. The 15hp model did not last long and was not listed as available at the start of 1924. The other models were re-designated B1 and B2 respectively. Later in the year the company decided to cease production of road vehicles and return solely to what they knew best - heavy machinery.

A cutaway illustration of a 7392cc Ruston 6YDA air cooled diesel engine. Originally designed as a stationary engine to power generators, pumps etc, one was modified and fitted into a Leyland bus for trials. The bus and engine still survive in the care of the Lincolnshire Vintage Vehicle Society. (Ray Hooley)

The company did however have a slight essay back into motor vehicles in 1959 when, as part of the Davey Paxman Group, they designed a 7.39 litre air cooled diesel engine which was fitted into a Leyland bus, which is now in the care of the Lincolnshire Vintage Vehicle Society on Whisby Road in Lincoln.

Approximately 1300 cars were made by Ruston & Hornsby and twenty are known to survive, twelve being in Great Britain and a further eight in Australia. However given the fact that many cars were known to still be in daily use up until the 1950's, in such places as India and the Canary Islands, there are probably more waiting to be found.

The company has survived but changed it name many times and has been owned by several different companies. It is now owned by Siemens and manufactures gas turbine engines for generating electricity.

Shelsley Motors Ltd, Bourne

See Raymond Mays

Stonebow, Lincoln

Marketed by R M Wright from his premises in Water Lane in Lincoln, the Stonebow car was purely an exercise in 'badge engineering'.

R.M. Wright's real name was A G Dykes, who had been a professional cycle racer. Unfortunately his family disapproved of such activities, hence the pseudonym of R M Wright, which allowed him to continue his cycling career. In 1890 he set up a bicycle sales and repair business, and was soon selling the Stonebow range of bicycles. The Stonebow cars, sold from 1900 to 1901 were in fact made by Payne and Bates of Coventry and were fitted with 5hp Aster engines.

The company name of R M Wright lived on until recently, synonymous in Lincolnshire with the sales of BMC/British Leyland/Rover Group cars, and only disappeared with the demise of Rover.

Sylva Autokits, Mablethorpe, Louth, Bardney, Hagworthingham, Horncastle

Sylva Autokits was set up in 1981 by draughtsman Jeremy Phillips, in order to manufacture his newly designed kit car, the Sylva Star. Best described as a modern interpretation of the classic Lotus Seven, it used a tubular steel space frame chassis with stressed sheet steel panelling and fibreglass body panels. Engine options included Fiat twin cam and Ford cross flow, but the other mechanical components were taken from either a Vauxhall Viva, Magnum, Firenza or Chevette. Some of these components required modification before fitting. Production started in 1982 in Mablethorpe, and in 1983 the all GRP bodied Leader was added to the range. The introduction of the Leader coincided with production moving to Lymington in Hampshire.

In 1985 the Striker Mark1 made it's debut. Based around a Leader chassis it was fitted with a Ford Escort rear axle and a Mazda 10a rotary engine.

In 1986 the Mark 2 version of the Striker and the Striker Clubman were introduced. These had a new space frame chassis designed for Ford Escort components. In order to concentrate on Striker development the Star and Leader projects were both sold to Swindon Sportscars.

Sylva Leader (Sylva Autokits)

86

1987 saw Sylva production return to Lincolnshire, this time in Louth, and the following year the budget Mark 3 Striker was released. This used a GRP transmission tunnel and Vauxhall Chevette front uprights. The Mark 3 was the first Sylva car to use outboard suspension. 1988 also saw the introduction of the Striker Mark 4 which used an all-enveloping GRP body as opposed to the basic Lotus Seven types offered previously. The Mark 4, later known as the Phoenix, was such a successful package that examples of it won eight out of ten of the 750 Motor Club's Kit Car Championships during the 1990's!

Sylva Phoenix (Sylva Autokits)

In 1991 the Fury was announced. This used a modified Mark 4 body, and looked very much like an archetypal classic British 1960's sports car. A one piece bonnet and front wings, similar to the Triumph Spitfire, allowed excellent access to the engine and mechanicals. The newly designed space frame chassis was designed for Ford Escort Mark 1 or 2 components. The Fury project was sold to Fisher Sportscars in 1994, so that the company could concentrate on the new Stylus.

The Stylus was an evolution of the Fury but used a one piece GRP body and conventional lift up bonnet. A steel tube space frame chassis and stressed sheet metal panels was used, and the design allowed fitment of a Ford Sierra rear axle, giving independent rear suspension. The Stylus was also the first Sylva to have a boot!

In 1996 the new Jester was introduced, so in keeping with Sylva's usual policy, the Stylus project was sold off, to Specialist Sports Cars of Woking in Surrey. The Jester was a small open fun car, best described as a modern beach buggy. The design really came about due to the big motor manufacturers deciding that front wheel drive was the way to go for ordinary motoring. This meant less suitable donors for the kit car industry, which had always favoured rear wheel drive. The front wheel drive Jester led the way for the industry, using the components from the Ford Fiesta bolted to a space frame chassis. Even the Fiesta interior was used! Sylva manufactured the kit until 1998 when it was sold to Harlequin Autokits.

1999 brought a revised Phoenix body and the following year another new car in the shape of the Mojo. This car used a space frame chassis and most of it's components from a Ford Fiesta. But unlike the Jester this car used the Fiesta engine, gearbox and drive train mounted behind the driver, in the middle of the car, so giving rear wheel drive and superb weight distribution giving better handling.

In 2001 a new factory was set up in Bardney and the Phoenix was sold to Stuart Taylor Motorsport. The following year saw Raw Engineering of Hereford acquire the Striker project and updated version of the Mojo being announced. The Mojo 2 featured a re-designed rear end and completely independent suspension. Engine options now included Ford Ka, Focus or Puma. However some problems occurred, particularly during racing, as the larger, heavier engines such as the Ford CVH and early Zetec tended to slightly unbalance the car. Also the 750 Motor Club, who organise Kit Car racing, deemed that a mid-engined layout was too much of an advantage, so the Mojo was moved to the toughest racing class, regardless of engine fitted. Therefore the company took the decision to suspend racing activities and concentrate on developing the Mojo 2 as a serious road car, which resulted in revised styling in 2003.

However, as can be expected from a company used to producing such successful sports cars, the call of racing once again became strong. This resulted in the R1ot being announced in 2004. The arrival of the new design coincided with the company's move to a new factory in Hagworthingham. The R1ot uses a Mojo 2 space frame, in which the cockpit has been moved forward to allow more room in the rear

Sylva R1ot fitted with a Yamaha R1 engine (Sylva Autokits)

Sylva Riot Mk 2 (Sylva Autokits)

engine bay. Moving the driver forward also helps with the car's weight distribution. The engine chosen was from the Yamaha R1 motorcycle which was transversely mounted in a specially designed cradle. Other cradles could be used to allow fitment of different engines. Drive was taken via a chain from the motorcycle gearbox to a sprocket bolted to a standard Fiesta differential unit mounted in a specially made carrier.

Standard Fiesta driveshafts transmitted the power to the rear wheels. The Mojo GRP body was dispensed with in favour of a simple aluminium skinned chassis and GRP nose cone. The front of the chassis was also re-designed to allow the fitment of inboard suspension. To allow different engines to be fitted a long wheelbase version is also offered.

In 2005 the Riot SE was announced. Basically this is a R1ot chassis fitted with a Ford Zetec SE engine. As this engine is all alloy, and the drivers cockpit is now further forward, there are none of the problems associated with the earlier, heavier units. In fact the weight balance is now 60/40% giving superb handling characteristics. The Riot SE was awarded the title of Kit Car of the Year 2005 by Which Kit Car? Magazine.

In 2006 all sales, marketing and support was taken on by Steve Knee and Matt Perrins of Stingray Motorsport in Ripley, Derbyshire. Kit production and development was moved to a new factory in Horncastle, still under the control of Jeremy Phillips.

Sylva Mojo 2 (Sylva Autokits)

Tomcat Motorsport, Skellingthorpe

Tomcat 100" (Tomcat Motorsport)

In 1984 Drew Bowler from Belper in Derbyshire fitted coil springs and a 2.2 litre twin cam engine to an 88" wheelbase Land-Rover for use in off road motor sport events. This proved so successful that in 1986 he converted a Land-Rover to a similar specification for his first paying customer. In 1989 he designed the Tomcat 88" which was sold as a kit and used a Land-Rover chassis and a tubular steel cage, on to which were mounted Land-Rover components and fibreglass body panels. In 1995 the Tomcat 100" was introduced, followed by the full spaceframe Wildcat in 1997.

In 2001 Bowler decided to concentrate on the Wildcat design and the production of Tomcat kits was taken on by Paul Williamson and Steve Wells who set up Tomcat Motorsport in Skellingthorpe. This company has since developed two new models and there are currently five vehicles in the Tomcat range. The first two are the 93 which uses a Land-Rover 90 chassis and the 106 which is designed for high speed events and can have the engine mounted in the front or rear of the vehicle.

Rolling chassis and cage for a Tomcat 100 inch. (Tomcat Motorsport)

Tomcat undergoing test of axle articulation! (Tomcat Motorsport)

The most popular model is the 100 and uses either a Range Rover or Discovery chassis. As well as for competitions this vehicle is also popular for road use. The 88 is advertised as a good comp safari or trials competitor and finally there is the 80 which is mainly aimed at off road trials due to it's short wheelbase and light weight.

In 2003 another partner, Ian Frame, joined Tomcat and another company was purchased to allow the Skellingthorpe firm to produce their own fibreglass bodywork.

Other products are also offered including quick ratio steering boxes, axle strengthening kits and GRP dashboards.

Torpedo, Barton upon Humber

See Elswick-Hopper

Traveller, Goole, Lincs/Yorks Border

William Shaw of Aire Street, Goole is recorded as making cars that boasted front wheel drive, sometime between 1900 and 1910. Nothing else known.

White's Imperial, Boston

Edward White of Bargate, Boston is recorded as making cars sometime between 1900 and 1910. Nothing else known.

Bourne Motor Racing Memorial

In November 2003 a memorial commemorating the contribution made by Raymond Mays and the town of Bourne to the world of motor racing was unveiled by David Owen, the chairman of Rubery Owen Holdings Limited, and Louis Stanley, former chairman and managing director of BRM. Situated on South Street in the town it features a stone plinth with a bronze plaque with the following inscription:

To commemorate the motor racing heritage of Bourne, celebrating the centenary of the birth of Raymond Mays CBE (1899-1980). A veritable giant of motor sport, he put the town on the world map of motor racing.

65 Years of ERA (1934-1999)

These voiturette racers became renowned worldwide for success in the classes for which they were designed and built, successes which continued into the 21st century with Historic Events.

50 Years of BRM (1949-1999)

The natural successor to the ERA, the BRM was aimed at the Formula One World Championships in a determined effort to put British cars in the front line of racing. In 1962, Graham Hill OBE won the Formula One Drivers' World Championship in the P57/8 model. This brought the Formula One Constructors' World Championship to the town. Testament to the dedication and professionalism of a workforce comprised mainly of local people. The company was acquired by the Rubery Owen Group on the 1st of November 1952. Sir Alfred and Ernest Owen, along with their sister Mrs Jean Stanley, took much personal interesting it's running. Mrs Stanley and husband Louis later assumed full management of the company.

On 29th August 1999, Bourne saw the return of cars associated with the town. The occasion was marked with a celebration dinner and roads were closed off to allow demonstrations of the racing cars.

This memorial was financed with the proceeds of this event.

The bronze plaque features a portrait of Raymond Mays, flanked by the ERA and BRM logos, and an ERA and BRM car. The BRM is representative of the car raced by Graham Hill.

The Bourne event in 1999 is still fresh in the author's mind to this day, memorable for the spirited driving of the cars and the several days of ringing in the ears caused by the sound of un-silenced racing car exhausts echoing around the narrow streets! And I loved every minute!

NOT MADE IN LINCOLNSHIRE!

W hile I was researching this book I came across some vehicles that have in the past been thought of by some as made in Lincolnshire, but in reality have no connection with the county whatsoever. Whilst listing Lincolnshire's makers I thought correcting some myths was also worth doing.

Elswick cars

The assets of the Elswick Cycle Company of Newcastle were bought in 1910 by Fred Hopper of Barton on Humber, to form the Elswick-Hopper Cycle and Motor Company. Between 1903 and 1907 Elswick of Newcastle had marketed a range of cars from a 6hp De Dion engined light car to a 24/30 four cylinder model. They sometimes carried the initials S.P.Q.R. which is well known to historians of the Roman period as standing for Senatus Populusque Romanum which, translated from the Latin means 'People and Senate of Rome'.

Gwynne cars

The Gwynne company was started in 1849 and specialised in the manufacture of centrifugal pumps from a factory in Hammersmith in West London. During the First World War the company set up a special factory, also in London, for the production of aircraft engines. In 1919, in order to keep the aircraft engine factory busy, Gwynne's started to manufacture car engines for Adam, Grimaldi & Co Ltd, for their Albert car. Unfortunately in 1920 Adam, Grimaldi defaulted on a payment to Gwynne's and shortly afterwards found themselves owned by their engine supplier. In 1922 the first car to carry the Gwynne name was introduced, as was the Gwynne-Albert 14hp. However the following year the company hit financial trouble and the Albert range of cars was dropped. The company decided to concentrate on production of the Gwynne Eight and Fourteen models only. In 1925 Gwynne Cars Ltd was sold by it's parent company and continued in production until 1929.

The confusion with Lincoln starts in 1927 when Gwynne's Pumps Limited was bought by William Foster & Co Ltd, and all production of industrial pumps transferred to Foster's Firth Road factory. Once they had been sold by their parent company (Gwynne's Engineering Co Ltd) their was no further connection between the car and pump making companies.

Lincoln cars

As well as the Ford owned Lincoln Motor Company, which is well known as a prestige American maker of presidential limousines, there have also been five other US makers using the Lincoln name, going back to the year 1900. There has also been an Australian made Lincoln car which was manufactured between 1919 and 1926.

However the car which causes the confusion is the British made Lincoln, which was manufactured by the Field and Slater company of Liverpool in 1920. These three wheeled cars were powered by 8hp Blackburn engines and had three speed gearboxes. As well as Liverpool these cars were also marketed from an address in Lancaster Gardens, Ealing, West London.

Pick motorcycles

In the May 1991 issue of the 'Classic Motorcycle' magazine, the highly respected motoring historian Michael Worthington-Williams had an article published about a newly restored Pick motorcycle, which was fitted with a 5/6hp Dalm engine. Instinct would point to Pick of Stamford being the maker. However, Michael Key, author of the excellent book 'Pick of Stamford', points out that during his research into the company no evidence was found of any motorcycles being made. The nearest came when he found out that an employee of Pick's, one W. Edinborough, had constructed a motorcycle for his own use. Other evidence of it not being Stamford made includes a Leicestershire registration number, and a transfer on the tank for the 'Leicester Cycle Company'. Michael Key's suggestion is that it was in fact made by the Leicester bicycle maker Henry Pick, who had a factory in that city from 1900 to 1927. During my research I too have not found any evidence of a Stamford made Pick motorcycle.

GLOSSARY AND DEFINITIONS

Brougham
Named after it's horse drawn forbear, this type of car body had a very distinct passenger compartment, totally separate from that of the driver. In the earliest versions the driving compartment was open to the elements, with the passengers in the warm and dry. Later versions gave cover to the driver but the distinction between chauffer and passenger were highlighted in other ways, such as the passenger compartment being wider than that of the driver, and even to the extent of retaining it's own carriage lamps.

De Dion Axle
A system of final drive in which the drive is transmitted to each driving wheel via a back axle with independent half shafts, fitted with universal joints. Named after the French De Dion-Bouton company, who first used the system on their steam powered cars in the 1890's.

Dickey-seat
An additional seat or seats fitted below a lift up lid on an open two-seater car. Most popular in the 1920's.

Free engine clutch
Basically a clutch to disconnect drive from the engine while it is still running. On early motorcycles with no gearboxes or clutch there was no 'neutral' gear, so you had to turn off the engine to stop.

J.A.P.
Also known simply as JAP. This stood for John. A. Prestwich, a manufacturer of engines and motorcycles based in Tottenham, London. After 1908 they concentrated their efforts on making engines and components for other manufacturers. In today's parlance JAP tends only to mean Japanese. Ironically in the early 1900's JAP actually drew a comparison themselves in one of their adverts by saying 'Japanese battleships are a striking success, and so are JAP motors!' Given the present Japanese dominance of the motor industry, I wonder what the Edwardian directors of JAP would think today!

Landaulet/Landaulette

A style of car body popular until just after World War One, in which only the rear section of the roof could be folded down.

Surface carburettor

An early form of carburettor in which the fuel is dripped onto a small metal plate, over which the inlet air is drawn. Fuel vapour is thus mixed with the air and drawn into the cylinder.

Tonneau

An early term for an open passenger carrying car body. Actually comes from the French word for a barrel! Entrance for the rear passengers was often through a door in the rear, between the seats. The name lives on in tonneau-cover, which is a cover for keeping the insides of a convertible sports car dry, without having to raise the roof.

Trembler coil

A very early form of electrical ignition using an induction coil and electromagnetic vibrator, which breaks the primary circuit and induces a high tension current in its secondary windings, producing a spark at the spark plug in the cylinder and igniting the fuel.

BIBLIOGRAPHY AND
RECOMMENDED READING

Clark R, Steam Engine Builders of Lincolnshire, The Society for Lincolnshire History and Archaeology, Lincoln, 1998

Cowbourne D, British Trial Drivers, Their Cars, Motorcycles and Awards 1902-1914, Westbury Publishing, Otley, West Yorkshire, 2003

Georgano N (Editor in Chief), The Beaulieu Encyclopedia of the Automobile, Volumes 1 & 2, The Stationary Office Ltd, Norwich, 2000

Good K, The House of Gwynne, Cars, Pumps & Aeroengines 1849-1968, Bookmarque Publishing, 2002

History of Saxilby & District Group, Step Back in Time, Saxilby cum Ingleby, Lincolnshire, History of Saxilby & District Group, Lincoln, 2005

Honeybone M, The Book Of Grantham, Barracuda Books Ltd, Buckingham, 1980

Howard J & Lester C (Editors), Lincolnshire on the Move, Society for Lincolnshire History and Archaeology, Lincoln, 2005

Key M, Pick Of Stamford, A History of the Pick Motor Company, Paul Watkins, Stamford, 1994

McGregor M, Raymond Mays of Bourne, Published by the author, Bourne, 1994.

Miller D, The Illustrated Encyclopedia of Trucks and Buses, Hamlyn Publishing Group Ltd, Middlesex, 1982

Mills D (Editor), History of Lincolnshire Volume X11, Twentieth Century Lincolnshire, The History of Lincolnshire Committee, Lincoln, 1989

Newman B, One Hundred Years of Good Company, The Story of Ruston & Hornsby, Northumberland Press Ltd, Gateshead on Tyne, 1957

Nye D, Famous Racing Cars, Guild Publishing, London, 1989

Prichard A, The Motor Racing Merchants, Leslie Frewin Publishers Ltd, London, 1976

Rudd T, It was fun! My fifty years of high performance, Patrick Stephens Ltd, Haynes Publishing Group, Sparkford, Somerset, 1993.

The Society of Motor Manufacturers and Traders, The Automobile Show, Crystal Palace, January 30th to February 7th, 1903, Patrick Stephens Ltd, Cambridge, 1973

Tragatsch E (Editor), The Illustrated Encyclopedia of Motorcycles, Hamlyn Publishing Group Ltd, Middlesex, 1977